At All Times and in All Places

Simon Jones is Chaplain and Fellow of Merton College, Oxford, and also teaches liturgy in the Faculty of Theology in the University of Oxford and at St Stephen's House, Oxford. He is editor of *The Sacramental Life: Gregory Dix and his Writings*, published by SCM-Canterbury Press, co-editor of *The Serious Business of Worship: Essays in Honour of Bryan D. Spinks*, published by T&T Clark, and co-author of *Celebrating the Eucharist, Celebrating Christ's Appearing* and *Celebrating Christ's Victory*, published by SPCK. He is a member of the Church of England Liturgical Commission.

At All Times and in All Places

Prayers and Readings for Themed Celebrations of the Eucharist

Compiled by
Simon Jones

CANTERBURY PRESS
Norwich

© Simon Jones 2014

First published in 2014 by the Canterbury Press Norwich
Editorial office
3rd Floor, Invicta House,
108–114 Golden Lane,
London EC1Y 0TG

Canterbury Press is an imprint of Hymns Ancient & Modern Ltd
(a registered charity)
13A Hellesdon Park Road, Norwich,
Norfolk NR6 5DR, UK

www.canterburypress.co.uk

All rights reserved. No part of this publication may be reproduced,
stored in a retrieval system, or transmitted,
in any form or by any means, electronic, mechanical,
photocopying or otherwise, without the prior permission of
the publisher, Canterbury Press.

The Author has asserted his right under the Copyright, Designs and
Patents Act, 1988, to be identified as the Author of this Work

Prayers and psalms are from *Common Worship: Services and Prayers for the Church of England* (2000), *Common Worship: Times and Seasons* (2006), *Common Worship: Times and Seasons, President's Edition* (2010) and *Common Worship: Festivals* (2008), are copyright © The Archbishops' Council and are reproduced by permission.

Scripture quotations are from the New Revised Standard Version of the Bible, Anglicized Edition, copyright 1989, 1995 by the Division of Christian Education of the National Council of the Churches of Christ in the USA. Used by permission. All rights reserved.

British Library Cataloguing in Publication data

A catalogue record for this book is available
from the British Library

978 1 84825 043 7

Typeset by Regent Typesetting
Printed and bound by
T.J. International, Cornwall

Contents

Acknowledgements   vii
Introduction   ix

Part One The Church and its Life   1

  1 The Holy Trinity   3
  2 The Holy Spirit   8
  3 The Holy Cross   13
  4 The Holy Name of Jesus   18
  5 The Sacred Heart of Jesus   23
       Year A   24
       Year B   28
       Year C   32
  6 Holy Baptism   37
  7 The Holy Eucharist   42
  8 The Blessed Virgin Mary   47
  9 Our Lady of Walsingham   52
10 All Saints   57
11 The Holy Angels   62
12 Christian Unity   68
13 Mission of the Church   73
14 Vocations   78

Part Two The Global and Local Community   83

15   The Environment   85
16   The Peace of the World   90
17   The Global Community (One World)   95
18   Those in Authority   101
19   Social Justice and Responsibility   106
20   Reconciliation   111
21   The Sovereign and Our National Life   116
22   Education   121
23   The Medical Profession   126

Part Three Pastoral Ministry   131

24   Thanksgiving for Marriage   133
25   The Sick and Suffering   138
26   The Bereaved   142
27   The Homeless   148
28   Victims of Natural Disaster   153
29   Victims of War and Conflict   158
30   The Departed   164

Resources   171
Acknowledgements   173

Acknowledgements

I owe a huge debt of gratitude to Michael Tavinor, Dean of Hereford, who, as my training incumbent, suggested that I might produce a collection of votives for use at weekday celebrations of the Eucharist at Tewkesbury Abbey, and commented on early drafts. I am also grateful to Christine Smith, of SCM-Canterbury Press, for her enthusiasm for the project, and for her patience in giving me time to complete it. Above all, my thanks are due to the Christian communities at Tewkesbury and Merton, with whom I have been privileged to celebrate the Eucharist, and who have reminded me of the importance of giving thanks to God 'at all times and in all places'.

Introduction

Votives for the contemporary Church

In the most well-known of his purple passages, Dom Gregory Dix, the Benedictine liturgist of the last century, emphasizes the universal and all-encompassing nature of the Eucharist:

> Was ever another command so obeyed? For century after century, spreading slowly to every continent and country and among every race of each, this action has been done, in every conceivable human circumstance, for every conceivable human need. (Dix, 1945, p. 743)

This book is designed to help the Church regain confidence in celebrating the Eucharist in every circumstance and for every need. In so doing, it draws on the western tradition of votive masses. Derived from the Latin *votum*, a votive mass is offered for a particular need or intention, or to celebrate a devotional theme. Though never an official part of the worshipping life of the Church of England, recent liturgical revisions have provided themed sets of readings and prayers for a small number of 'Special Occasions', such as for 'The Guidance of the Holy Spirit' and 'The Peace of the World' (see, for example, *Common Worship: Festivals*, pp. 332–67).

This collection includes a number of traditional votive themes and intentions which still find a place within the

Roman Catholic tradition, such as 'The Blessed Virgin Mary' and 'The Departed', to which are added a number of contemporary subjects. The thirty votives are divided into three sections: the first contains many of the traditional themes that relate to the Church and its life; the second provides material that looks outside the Church to the global and local community; and the third responds to pastoral concerns and the needs of those who suffer.

When to use a votive

The liturgical material in each votive has been compiled for use at the Eucharist, but it may also provide the Collect and Readings for a Service of the Word. It can be used in a number of different ways, including the following.

1. Weekday celebrations of the Eucharist. *Common Worship: Festivals* and *Exciting Holiness* (Tristam, 2003) provide appropriate material for Festivals and Lesser Festivals. On *ferias*, the occasional use of themed celebrations may be preferred to the semi-continuous pattern of readings provided by the Daily Eucharistic Lectionary (DEL). For example, in churches that normally have one weekday Eucharist, and the congregation will not hear the previous or following day's readings from the DEL; also, in churches that have a more frequent or even a daily pattern of eucharistic worship, but each service attracts a different congregation. In either case, so that the votives do not detract from the overall character of the seasons of the Church's Year, it may be appropriate to use them less frequently and more selectively in seasons, or to restrict their use to Ordinary Time.

INTRODUCTION

2 When it is desirable to highlight a particular theme or intention. For example, the tradition of having a votive of the Blessed Virgin Mary on Saturdays, a monthly requiem, or a Eucharist for healing with the laying on of hands and anointing as part of the regular worshipping life of the community.

3 In response to an international, national, or local event. Some of the material provided here is appropriate for use when a church wants to respond liturgically to a natural disaster, an act of terrorism, or a local tragedy in which people have been killed or injured.

4 On a Sunday that does not require the use of authorized lectionary provision. *Common Worship* states that, during Ordinary Time, 'authorized lectionary provision remains the norm but, after due consultation with the Parochial Church Council, the minister may, from time to time, depart from the lectionary provision for pastoral reasons or preaching or teaching purposes' (*Common Worship: Services and Prayers for the Church of England*, p. 540). In churches that always use authorized lectionary provision at the principal service, it may be appropriate to use a votive at another Sunday service.

How to use a votive

The liturgical material for each votive is prefaced by a brief introduction, sometimes giving guidance on when it may be used, and a suggested liturgical colour. Each contains a Collect, Reading(s) and Responsorial Psalm, Gospel Acclamation and Gospel Reading, Prayer over the Gifts, and Prayer after Communion. Many of the prayers have been written for this collection; the rest have been taken or adapted from Anglican and other sources.

This collection does not include entrance antiphons or communion sentences. If they are required, they may be taken from the passages of scripture provided. Nor does it contain prefaces for the Eucharistic Prayer (with the exception of the votive of the Sacred Heart). Where appropriate texts are available in *Common Worship*, these are referred to in the introduction. At a celebration using *Common Worship* Order 1 in modern language, the most appropriate volume for use on the altar-table is *Common Worship: Times and Seasons, President's Edition for Holy Communion* or, where indicated, *Common Worship: Festivals*.

It is hoped that by not providing texts to introduce the confession and peace, and forms of intercession, the president and other liturgical ministers will be encouraged to use their own words, appropriate to the occasion. At the beginning of the rite, whether the president uses a set form or improvises, it is important that the votive is introduced. So as not to overload the Gathering, this may follow the Greeting or Collect of Purity and be combined with the introduction to the confession. For example, in a votive for those in authority:

As we offer this Eucharist for those in positions of leadership, let us remember those ways in which we fail to live our lives in obedience to Christ's just and gentle rule.

Collect

Whereas in *Common Worship*, Sunday Collects are rarely tied to particular sets of readings, the opening prayers provided in this collection relate explicitly to the theme of the votive. There are four elements to the Collect: the bidding, silent prayer, Collect and 'Amen'. At a votive Eucharist, a more extended form of bidding may be preferred to 'Let us pray'. For example, at a votive of the Holy Spirit: 'Let us pray that our lives may be transformed by the power of the Spirit'.

Readings

The biblical readings and psalm have been chosen with the theme of each votive in mind and, within the collection, try to give broad coverage of the Old Testament, Apocrypha, and New Testament. Each set contains a Gospel Acclamation. Wherever possible, it should be sung to a simple tone, even at a said service. In Lent, 'Alleluia' is replaced by an alternative acclamation, such as 'Praise to you, O Christ, king of eternal glory'. It is appropriate for the deacon or priest reading the Gospel to greet the people with the words:

The Lord be with you
and also with you.

before introducing the reading.

Prayer over the Gifts

The Prayer over the Gifts (referred to in *Common Worship* as a 'Prayer at the Preparation of the Table') concludes the offertory and acts as a bridge between the preparation of the altar-table and the Eucharistic Prayer. One of its traditional functions is to emphasize the sacrificial nature of the eucharistic offering. A helpful description of what this might mean for Anglicans can be found in the 1971 ARCIC (Anglican-Roman Catholic International Commission) statement on the Eucharist:

In the Eucharistic Prayer the Church continues to make a perpetual memorial of Christ's death, and its members, united with God and one another, give thanks for all his mercies, entreat the benefits of his passion on behalf of the whole Church, participate in these benefits and enter into the movement of his self offering. (Hill and Yarnold, 1994, p. 20)

In this collection, the Prayer over the Gifts points forward to this entry into the movement of Christ's self-offering in the Eucharistic Prayer by relating it to the theme of the votive. For example, in the votive of the Holy Trinity, the nexus between the sacrifice of the Eucharist and the sacrifice of Christ is articulated in this prayer, which draws on the *Te Deum*:

> Father of majesty unbounded,
> through the bread and wine we bless and share,
> make our offering one with the sacrifice of Christ,
>   your true and only Son,
> that in the power of the Spirit, our advocate and guide,
> we may bless and praise your name for ever.
> We ask this through Christ our Lord.

For Anglican Catholics, often frustrated by the inability of the Eucharistic Prayers of the Prayer Book and *Common Worship* to give voice to this essential aspect of Catholic eucharistic theology, these prayers are intended to compensate for what is lacking, while remaining within the boundaries of ARCIC, and not falling into the liturgical trap of anticipating what is about to happen in the Eucharistic Prayer. For others, for whom such an emphasis is theologically unacceptable, the Prayer over the Gifts is optional and may be omitted.

Where such a prayer is used, the president's hands are held in the *orans* position, as for the Collect. It may be prefaced with 'Let us pray', unless it is preceded by the following dia-

INTRODUCTION

logue (the *orate fratres*) from the Roman Rite, which further emphasizes the sacrificial nature of the Eucharist:

> Pray, brothers and sisters,
> that my sacrifice and yours
> may be acceptable to God,
> the almighty Father.
> **May the Lord accept the sacrifice at your hands**
> **for the praise and glory of his name,**
> **for our good**
> **and the good of all his holy Church.**

Prayer after Communion

Related to the theme of the votive, in giving thanks for the Eucharist the Prayer after Communion looks forward to the dismissal, highlighting the significance of being sent out from the worshipping community by focusing on the implications of the Eucharist for the Christian life. For example, in the votive for the homeless:

> God our refuge,
> we thank you for feeding us at your table
> with gifts of grace and goodness:
> may we who are now sent out in your name
> stand alongside the homeless and dispossessed
> and enable them to find shelter
>   under the shadow of your wings;
> through Jesus Christ our Lord.

Given the stress on dismissal in the majority of these texts, a congregational prayer following the president's Prayer after Communion will not always be necessary, and should always be omitted if it repeats what has already been said. Like the Collect, the Prayer after Communion has four elements. It is common for the silence to be quite short (particularly if a more extended period of silence is observed after the administration of Holy Communion), but it should not be omitted altogether.

Simon Jones
Merton College, Oxford
October 2013

PART ONE

The Church and its Life

I

The Holy Trinity

In this celebration we give thanks for God's self-revelation as Father, Son and Holy Spirit, and respond to his call to share his mission in the world, that the whole earth may resound with the glory of his praise.

*In addition to the texts provided here, material for use on Trinity Sunday may also be used (*Common Worship: Times and Seasons, *pp. 506–13;* Common Worship: Times and Seasons, President's Edition for Holy Communion, *pp. 284–91).*

The liturgical colour is white.

COLLECT

> Father of glory,
> you have called us to share in the life that is yours
> with your Son and the Holy Spirit:
> strengthen that life within your Church,
> that we may respond to your call,
> observe your commands,
> and proclaim the gospel to every nation;
> through Jesus Christ your Son our Lord,
> who is alive and reigns with you,
> in the unity of the Holy Spirit,
> one God, now and for ever.

READING   Isaiah 6.1–8

A reading from the prophecy of Isaiah.

> In the year that King Uzziah died, I saw the Lord sitting on a throne, high and lofty; and the hem of his robe filled the temple. Seraphs were in attendance above him; each had six wings: with two they covered their faces, and with two they covered their feet, and with two they flew. And one called to another and said:
>   'Holy, holy, holy is the Lord of hosts;
>   the whole earth is full of his glory.'
> The pivots on the thresholds shook at the voices of those who called, and the house filled with smoke. And I said: 'Woe is me! I am lost, for I am a man of unclean lips, and I live among a people of unclean lips; yet my eyes have seen the King, the Lord of hosts!'

Then one of the seraphs flew to me, holding a live coal that had been taken from the altar with a pair of tongs. The seraph touched my mouth with it and said: 'Now that this has touched your lips, your guilt has departed and your sin is blotted out.' Then I heard the voice of the Lord saying, 'Whom shall I send, and who will go for us?' And I said, 'Here am I; send me!'

This is the word of the Lord.

PSALM 29.1–4, 7–end

O worship the Lord in the beauty of holiness.
All **O worship the Lord in the beauty of holiness.**

Ascribe to the Lord, you powers of heaven,
ascribe to the Lord glory and strength.
Ascribe to the Lord the honour due to his name;
worship the Lord in the beauty of holiness.
All **O worship the Lord in the beauty of holiness.**

The voice of the Lord is upon the waters;
    the God of glory thunders;
the Lord is upon the mighty waters.
The voice of the Lord is mighty in operation;
the voice of the Lord is a glorious voice.
All **O worship the Lord in the beauty of holiness.**

The voice of the Lord splits the flash of lightning;
the voice of the Lord shakes the wilderness;
   the Lord shakes the wilderness of Kadesh.
The voice of the Lord makes the oak trees writhe
   and strips the forests bare;
in his temple all cry, 'Glory!'
All **O worship the Lord in the beauty of holiness.**

The Lord sits enthroned above the water flood;
the Lord sits enthroned as king for evermore.
The Lord shall give strength to his people;
the Lord shall give his people the blessing of peace.
All **O worship the Lord in the beauty of holiness.**

ACCLAMATION

Alleluia. **Alleluia.**
Holy, holy, holy Lord, God of power and might:
heaven and earth are full of your glory.
Alleluia.

GOSPEL *Matthew 28.16–end*

Hear the Gospel of our Lord Jesus Christ according to Matthew.

The eleven disciples went to Galilee, to the mountain to which Jesus had directed them. When they saw him, they worshipped him; but some doubted. And Jesus came and said to them, 'All authority in heaven and on earth has been given to me. Go therefore and make disciples of all nations, baptizing them in the name of the Father and of the Son and of the Holy Spirit, and teaching them to obey everything that I have commanded you. And remember, I am with you always, to the end of the age.'

This is the Gospel of the Lord.

PRAYER OVER THE GIFTS

> Father of majesty unbounded,
> through the bread and wine we bless and share,
> make our offering one with the sacrifice of Christ,
>   your true and only Son,
> that in the power of the Spirit, our advocate and guide,
> we may bless and praise your name for ever.
> We ask this through Christ our Lord.

PRAYER AFTER COMMUNION

> Gracious and all-powerful God,
> may we who have shared in this Eucharist,
> worship you with thankful hearts
> and ever live to proclaim the glory of your name,
> who are three Persons yet one God,
> now and for ever.

2

The Holy Spirit

In this Eucharist we rejoice in the power of the Holy Spirit and invoke his renewing presence upon the life of the Church and the world. We give thanks for the gift of the Spirit received in baptism, which unites Christian people as one body in Christ, and pray that our hearts may be transformed by the fire of his love.

*In addition to the texts provided here, material for use from Ascension Day to Pentecost may also be used (*Common Worship: Times and Seasons, *pp. 483–9;* Common Worship: Times and Seasons, President's Edition for Holy Communion, *pp. 251–8).*

The liturgical colour is red.

THE HOLY SPIRIT

COLLECT

God, the giver of life,
whose Holy Spirit wells up within your Church:
by the Spirit's gifts equip us to live the gospel of Christ
    and make us eager to do your will,
that we may share with the whole creation
    the joys of eternal life;
through Jesus Christ your Son our Lord,
who is alive and reigns with you,
in the unity of the Holy Spirit,
one God, now and for ever.

READING *Romans 8.22–27*

A reading from the Letter of Paul to the Romans.

We know that the whole creation has been groaning in labour pains until now; and not only the creation, but we ourselves, who have the first fruits of the Spirit, groan inwardly while we wait for adoption, the redemption of our bodies. For in hope we were saved. Now hope that is seen is not hope. For who hopes for what is seen? But if we hope for what we do not see, we wait for it with patience.

Likewise the Spirit helps us in our weakness; for we do not know how to pray as we ought, but that very Spirit intercedes with sighs too deep for words. And God, who searches the heart, knows what is the mind of the Spirit, because the Spirit intercedes for the saints according to the will of God.

This is the word of the Lord.

AT ALL TIMES AND IN ALL PLACES

CANTICLE *Wisdom 9.1–5a, c, 6, 9–11*

    Send Wisdom forth from your holy heavens;
    from the throne of your glory send her.

All **Send Wisdom forth from your holy heavens;**
    from the throne of your glory send her.

    O God of our ancestors and Lord of mercy,
    you have made all things by your word.
    By your wisdom you have formed us
    to have dominion over the creatures you have made;
    To rule the world in holiness and righteousness
    and to pronounce judgement in uprightness of soul.

All **Send Wisdom forth from your holy heavens;**
    from the throne of your glory send her.

    Give us the Wisdom that sits by your throne;
    do not reject us from among your servants,
    For we are your servants,
    with little understanding of judgement and laws.
    Even one who is perfect among us
    will be regarded as nothing
       without the wisdom that comes from you.

All **Send Wisdom forth from your holy heavens;**
    from the throne of your glory send her.

    With you is Wisdom, she who knows your works,
    and was present when you made the world.
    She understands what is pleasing in your sight
    and what is right according to your commandments.
    Send her forth from the holy heavens,
    from the throne of your glory send her.

All **Send Wisdom forth from your holy heavens;**
    from the throne of your glory send her.

THE HOLY SPIRIT

That she may labour at our side
and that we may learn what is pleasing to you.
For she knows and understands all things,
she will guide us wisely in our actions
    and guard us with her glory.

All **Send Wisdom forth from your holy heavens;**
from the throne of your glory send her.

ACCLAMATION

Alleluia. **Alleluia.**
Come, Holy Spirit, fill the hearts
   of your faithful people:
and kindle in us the fire of your love.
Alleluia.

GOSPEL   *John 14.15–17, 25–26*

Hear the Gospel of our Lord Jesus Christ according to John.

Jesus said to Philip, 'If you love me, you will keep my commandments. And I will ask the Father, and he will give you another Advocate, to be with you for ever. This is the Spirit of truth, whom the world cannot receive, because it neither sees him nor knows him. You know him, because he abides with you, and he will be in you.

'I have said these things to you while I am still with you. But the Advocate, the Holy Spirit, whom the

Father will send in my name, will teach you everything,
and remind you of all that I have said to you.'

This is the Gospel of the Lord.

PRAYER OVER THE GIFTS

Holy Father,
giver of all good gifts,
accept this bread and cup
  which we offer you in thanksgiving:
by the power of your abiding Spirit,
renew your Church for service in the world,
and make us a perfect offering in your sight;
through Jesus Christ our Lord.

PRAYER AFTER COMMUNION

God of power,
whose Holy Spirit renews your people
in the bread and wine we bless and share:
may the boldness of the Spirit transform us,
the gentleness of the Spirit lead us,
and the gifts of the Spirit equip us to serve
  and worship you;
through Jesus Christ our Lord.

3

The Holy Cross

This votive celebrates the victory of the cross. Although the principal commemorations of the cross are Passiontide and Holy Cross Day (14 September), it is an appropriate thanksgiving at other times of the year, particularly on Fridays. In this Eucharist we give thanks for the salvation won for us at so great a cost and pledge ourselves to live as disciples of Christ crucified.

In addition to the texts provided here, material for use in Passiontide may also be used (Common Worship: Times and Seasons, pp. 260–7; Common Worship: Times and Seasons, President's Edition for Holy Communion, pp. 162–7); and on Holy Cross Day (Common Worship: Festivals, pp. 102–7).

The liturgical colour is red.

COLLECT

> Lifted up on the cross,
> your Son reconciled the world to you,
> our merciful Father:
> may all who experience your forgiveness
> > in Christ crucified
> proclaim the good news of your loving wisdom
> > and saving power;
> through him, to whom every knee shall bow,
> > Jesus our Lord,
> who is alive and reigns with you,
> in the unity of the Holy Spirit,
> one God, now and for ever.

READING   *1 Corinthians 1.18–25*

A reading from the First Letter of Paul to the Corinthians.

> The message about the cross is foolishness to those who are perishing, but to us who are being saved it is the power of God. For it is written,
> > 'I will destroy the wisdom of the wise,
> > and the discernment of the discerning I will thwart.'
> Where is the one who is wise? Where is the scribe? Where is the debater of this age? Has not God made foolish the wisdom of the world? For since, in the wisdom of God, the world did not know God through wisdom, God decided, through the foolishness of our proclamation, to save those who believe. For Jews demand signs and Greeks desire wisdom, but we proclaim Christ crucified,

THE HOLY CROSS

a stumbling-block to Jews and foolishness to Gentiles, but to those who are the called, both Jews and Greeks, Christ the power of God and the wisdom of God. For God's foolishness is wiser than human wisdom, and God's weakness is stronger than human strength.

This is the word of the Lord.

CANTICLE *Philippians 2.5–11*

At the name of Jesus every knee shall bow.
All **At the name of Jesus every knee shall bow.**

Christ Jesus was in the form of God,
but he did not cling to equality with God.
He emptied himself, taking the form of a servant,
and was born in our human likeness.
All **At the name of Jesus every knee shall bow.**

Being found in human form he humbled himself,
and became obedient unto death,
    even death on a cross.
Therefore God has highly exalted him,
and bestowed on him the name above every name,
All **At the name of Jesus every knee shall bow.**

That at the name of Jesus every knee should bow,
in heaven and on earth and under the earth;
And every tongue confess that Jesus Christ is Lord,
to the glory of God the Father.
All **At the name of Jesus every knee shall bow.**

ACCLAMATION

> Alleluia. **Alleluia.**
> We adore you, O Christ, and we bless you:
> because by your holy cross
>   you have redeemed the world.
> **Alleluia.**

GOSPEL Mark 15.25–39

Hear the Gospel of our Lord Jesus Christ according to Mark.

> It was nine o'clock in the morning when they crucified Jesus. The inscription of the charge against him read, 'The King of the Jews.' And with him they crucified two bandits, one on his right and one on his left. Those who passed by derided him, shaking their heads and saying, 'Aha! You who would destroy the temple and build it in three days, save yourself, and come down from the cross!' In the same way the chief priests, along with the scribes, were also mocking him among themselves and saying, 'He saved others; he cannot save himself. Let the Messiah, the King of Israel, come down from the cross now, so that we may see and believe.' Those who were crucified with him also taunted him.
> When it was noon, darkness came over the whole land until three in the afternoon. At three o'clock Jesus cried out with a loud voice, 'Eloi, Eloi, lema sabachthani?' which means, 'My God, my God, why have you forsaken me?' When some of the bystanders heard it, they said, 'Listen, he is calling for Elijah.' And someone ran, filled a sponge with sour wine, put it on a stick,

THE HOLY CROSS

and gave it to him to drink, saying, 'Wait, let us see whether Elijah will come to take him down.' Then Jesus gave a loud cry and breathed his last. And the curtain of the temple was torn in two, from top to bottom. Now when the centurion, who stood facing him, saw that in this way he breathed his last, he said, 'Truly this man was God's Son!'

This is the Gospel of the Lord.

PRAYER OVER THE GIFTS

> God of mercy,
> through the death of your beloved Son
> you transformed an instrument of shame
> into a sign of hope and glory:
> receive all we offer you this day
> and renew in us the mystery of his love;
> through the same Jesus Christ our Lord.

PRAYER AFTER COMMUNION

> Faithful God,
> whose Son bore our sins in his body on the tree
> and gave us this sacrament to show forth his death
>   until he comes:
> give us grace to glory in the cross
>   of our Lord Jesus Christ,
> for he is our salvation, our life and our hope,
> and reigns as Lord, now and for ever.

4

The Holy Name of Jesus

This votive acknowledges the saving power of the name of Jesus, literally, 'Yahweh saves'. Linked to the name by which God made himself known to Moses, 'I am who I am' (Exodus 3.14), the holy name of Jesus reveals the purpose of his existence and invites the devotion of those who find salvation in him.

In the calendar of the Book of Common Prayer, the Name of Jesus was commemorated on 7 August. In the Church of England it is now observed as part of the combined festival of the Naming and Circumcision of Christ on 1 January (and, in the Roman Catholic Church, as an optional memorial on 3 January). This votive is particularly appropriate in January.

*In addition to the texts provided here, material for use on the feast of the Naming and Circumcision of Jesus may also be used (*Common Worship: Festivals, *pp. 37–41).*

The liturgical colour is white.

THE HOLY NAME OF JESUS

COLLECT

> Eternal Father,
> who has taught that in the name of Jesus Christ alone
>   is our salvation:
> mercifully grant that your faithful people,
> ever glorying in his name,
> may make your salvation known to all the world;
> through the same Jesus Christ our Lord,
> who is alive and reigns with you,
> in the unity of the Holy Spirit,
> one God, now and for ever.

READING   *Acts 4.8–12*

A reading from the Acts of the Apostles.

> Peter, filled with the Holy Spirit, said, 'Rulers of the people and elders, if we are questioned today because of a good deed done to someone who was sick and are asked how this man has been healed, let it be known to all of you, and to all the people of Israel, that this man is standing before you in good health by the name of Jesus Christ of Nazareth, whom you crucified, whom God raised from the dead. This Jesus is
>   "the stone that was rejected by you, the builders;
>   it has become the cornerstone."
> There is salvation in no one else, for there is no other name under heaven given among mortals by which we must be saved.'

This is the word of the Lord.

PSALM 135.1–4, 13–14

Blessed be the name of the Lord.
All **Blessed be the name of the Lord.**

Praise the name of the Lord;
give praise, you servants of the Lord,
You that stand in the house of the Lord,
in the courts of the house of our God.
All **Blessed be the name of the Lord.**

Praise the Lord, for the Lord is good;
make music to his name, for it is lovely.
For the Lord has chosen Jacob for himself
and Israel for his own possession.
All **Blessed be the name of the Lord.**

Your name, O Lord, endures for ever
and shall be remembered through all generations.
For the Lord will vindicate his people
and have compassion on his servants.
All **Blessed be the name of the Lord.**

ACCLAMATION

Alleluia. **Alleluia.**
At the name of Jesus:
every knee shall bow.
Alleluia.

THE HOLY NAME OF JESUS

GOSPEL *Matthew 1.20–23*

Hear the Gospel of our Lord Jesus Christ according to Matthew.

> An angel of the Lord appeared to Joseph in a dream and said, 'Joseph, son of David, do not be afraid to take Mary as your wife, for the child conceived in her is from the Holy Spirit. She will bear a son, and you are to name him Jesus, for he will save his people from their sins.' All this took place to fulfil what had been spoken by the Lord through the prophet:
>   'Look, the virgin shall conceive and bear a son,
>   and they shall name him Emmanuel',
> which means, 'God is with us.'

This is the Gospel of the Lord.

PRAYER OVER THE GIFTS

> Holy Father,
> your Son is the cornerstone of our salvation:
> accept the gifts we bring before you as we celebrate
>   his saving sacrifice;
> may the offering of ourselves in his service bring
>   honour to his holy name,
> who is Lord for ever and ever.

PRAYER AFTER COMMUNION

> Everlasting God,
> whose Son, our Saviour, was given the name
>   above all other names:
> may our sharing in these holy mysteries
> deepen our love for him and for each other,
> that we may never doubt his power to heal and save,
> who is alive and reigns, now and for ever.

5

The Sacred Heart of Jesus

The feast of the Sacred Heart is celebrated on the Friday following the First Sunday after Trinity. Although it has never been commemorated in an official Church of England calendar, a celebration of the Divine Compassion of Christ on this day appeared in the Franciscan office book Celebrating Common Prayer *and is observed by a number of Anglican communities.*

The material provided here may be used on the feast itself (for which the Roman Catholic Church provides three sets of readings) or as a votive at another time in the year. Its connection with the Passion of Christ makes its use on Fridays particularly appropriate.

The liturgical colour is white. The Roman Catholic Church celebrates this feast as a Solemnity (with Gloria and Creed at the Eucharist) and provides three readings for each of the three years of the lectionary. At a votive, the Gospel may be preceded by one of the readings and the psalm from one of the sets of readings.

COLLECT

Almighty God,
whose Son, our Lord Jesus Christ,
was moved with compassion
   for all who had gone astray
and with indignation for all who had suffered wrong:
inflame our hearts with the burning fire of your love,
that we may seek out the lost,
have mercy on the fallen
and stand fast for truth and righteousness;
through Jesus Christ our Lord,
who is alive and reigns with you,
in the unity of the Holy Spirit,
one God, now and for ever.

YEAR A

READING   *Deuteronomy 7.6–11*

A reading from the Book of Deuteronomy.

You are a people holy to the Lord your God; the Lord your God has chosen you out of all the peoples on earth to be his people, his treasured possession.

It was not because you were more numerous than any other people that the Lord set his heart on you and chose you – for you were the fewest of all peoples. It was because the Lord loved you and kept the oath that he swore to your ancestors, that the LORD has brought you out with a mighty hand, and redeemed you from the house of slavery, from the hand of Pharaoh king of Egypt. Know therefore that the LORD your God is God, the faithful God who maintains covenant loyalty with those who love him and keep his commandments, to a thousand generations, and who repays in their own person those who reject him. He does not delay but repays in their own person those who reject him. Therefore, observe diligently the commandment – the statutes and the ordinances – that I am commanding you today.

This is the word of the Lord.

PSALM 103.1–4, 6–8, 10

The Lord is full of compassion and mercy.
All **The Lord is full of compassion and mercy.**

Bless the Lord, O my soul,
and all that is within me bless his holy name.
Bless the Lord, O my soul,
and forget not all his benefits.
All **The Lord is full of compassion and mercy.**

Who forgives all your sins
and heals all your infirmities;
Who redeems your life from the Pit
and crowns you with faithful love and compassion.
All **The Lord is full of compassion and mercy.**

The Lord executes righteousness
and judgement for all who are oppressed.
He made his ways known to Moses
and his works to the children of Israel.

All **The Lord is full of compassion and mercy.**

The Lord is full of compassion and mercy,
slow to anger and of great kindness.
He has not dealt with us according to our sins,
nor rewarded us according to our wickedness.

All **The Lord is full of compassion and mercy.**

READING   *1 John 4.7–16*

A reading from the First Letter of John.

Beloved, let us love one another, because love is from God; everyone who loves is born of God and knows God. Whoever does not love does not know God, for God is love. God's love was revealed among us in this way: God sent his only Son into the world so that we might live through him. In this is love, not that we loved God but that he loved us and sent his Son to be the atoning sacrifice for our sins. Beloved, since God loved us so much, we also ought to love one another. No one has ever seen God; if we love one another, God lives in us, and his love is perfected in us.

By this we know that we abide in him and he in us, because he has given us of his Spirit. And we have seen and do testify that the Father has sent his Son as the Saviour of the world. God abides in those who confess that Jesus is the Son of God, and they abide in God. So we have known and believe the love that God has for us.

God is love, and those who abide in love abide in God, and God abides in them.

This is the word of the Lord.

ACCLAMATION

Alleluia. **Alleluia.**
Take my yoke upon you, and learn from me:
and you will find rest for your souls.
Alleluia.

GOSPEL *Matthew 11.25–30*

Hear the Gospel of our Lord Jesus Christ according to Matthew.

Jesus said, 'I thank you, Father, Lord of heaven and earth, because you have hidden these things from the wise and the intelligent and have revealed them to infants; yes, Father, for such was your gracious will. All things have been handed over to me by my Father; and no one knows the Son except the Father, and no one knows the Father except the Son and anyone to whom the Son chooses to reveal him.

'Come to me, all you that are weary and are carrying heavy burdens, and I will give you rest. Take my yoke upon you, and learn from me; for I am gentle and humble in heart, and you will find rest for your souls. For my yoke is easy, and my burden is light.'

This is the Gospel of the Lord.

YEAR B

READING   *Hosea 11.1, 3–4, 8–9*

A reading from the prophecy of Hosea.

> When Israel was a child, I loved him,
>   and out of Egypt I called my son.
> It was I who taught Ephraim to walk,
>   I took them up in my arms;
>   but they did not know that I healed them.
> I led them with cords of human kindness,
>   with bands of love.
> I was to them like those
>   who lift infants to their cheeks.
>   I bent down to them and fed them.
> How can I give you up, Ephraim?
>   How can I hand you over, O Israel?
> How can I make you like Admah?
>   How can I treat you like Zeboiim?
> My heart recoils within me;
>   my compassion grows warm and tender.
> I will not execute my fierce anger;
>   I will not again destroy Ephraim;

for I am God and no mortal,
   the Holy One in your midst,
   and I will not come in wrath.

This is the word of the Lord.

CANTICLE *Isaiah 12.2–6*

With joy you will draw water
   from the wells of salvation.

All **With joy you will draw water**
from the wells of salvation.

'Behold, God is my salvation;
I will trust and will not be afraid;
For the Lord God is my strength and my song,
and has become my salvation.'

All **With joy you will draw water**
from the wells of salvation.

On that day you will say,
'Give thanks to the Lord, call upon his name;
Make known his deeds among the nations,
proclaim that his name is exalted.'

All **With joy you will draw water**
from the wells of salvation.

'Sing God's praises, who has triumphed gloriously;
let this be known in all the world.
Shout and sing for joy, you that dwell in Zion,
for great in your midst is the Holy One of Israel.'

All **With joy you will draw water**
from the wells of salvation.

READING *Ephesians 3.8–12, 14–19*

A reading from the Letter of Paul to the Ephesians.

> Although I, Paul, am the very least of all the saints, this grace was given to me to bring to the Gentiles the news of the boundless riches of Christ, and to make everyone see what is the plan of the mystery hidden for ages in God who created all things; so that through the church the wisdom of God in its rich variety might now be made known to the rulers and authorities in the heavenly places. This was in accordance with the eternal purpose that he has carried out in Christ Jesus our Lord, in whom we have access to God in boldness and confidence through faith in him.
>
> For this reason I bow my knees before the Father, from whom every family in heaven and on earth takes its name. I pray that, according to the riches of his glory, he may grant that you may be strengthened in your inner being with power through his Spirit, and that Christ may dwell in your hearts through faith, as you are being rooted and grounded in love. I pray that you may have the power to comprehend, with all the saints, what is the breadth and length and height and depth, and to know the love of Christ that surpasses knowledge, so that you may be filled with all the fullness of God.

This is the word of the Lord.

ACCLAMATION

> Alleluia. **Alleluia.**
> In this is love, not that we loved God
>   but that he loved us:
> and sent his Son to be the atoning sacrifice for our sins.
> **Alleluia.**

GOSPEL *John 19.31–37*

Hear the Gospel of our Lord Jesus Christ according to John.

> Since it was the day of Preparation, the Jews did not want the bodies left on the cross during the sabbath, especially because that sabbath was a day of great solemnity. So they asked Pilate to have the legs of the crucified men broken and the bodies removed. Then the soldiers came and broke the legs of the first and of the other who had been crucified with him. But when they came to Jesus and saw that he was already dead, they did not break his legs. Instead, one of the soldiers pierced his side with a spear, and at once blood and water came out. (He who saw this has testified so that you also may believe. His testimony is true, and he knows that he tells the truth.) These things occurred so that the scripture might be fulfilled, 'None of his bones shall be broken.' And again another passage of scripture says, 'They will look on the one whom they have pierced.'

This is the Gospel of the Lord.

YEAR C

READING *Ezekiel 34.11–16*

A reading from the prophecy of Ezekiel.

> Thus says the Lord God: I myself will search for my sheep, and will seek them out. As shepherds seek out their flocks when they are among their scattered sheep, so I will seek out my sheep. I will rescue them from all the places to which they have been scattered on a day of clouds and thick darkness. I will bring them out from the peoples and gather them from the countries, and will bring them into their own land; and I will feed them on the mountains of Israel, by the watercourses, and in all the inhabited parts of the land. I will feed them with good pasture, and the mountain heights of Israel shall be their pasture; there they shall lie down in good grazing land, and they shall feed on rich pasture on the mountains of Israel. I myself will be the shepherd of my sheep, and I will make them lie down, says the Lord God. I will seek the lost, and I will bring back the strayed, and I will bind up the injured, and I will strengthen the weak, but the fat and the strong I will destroy. I will feed them with justice.

This is the word of the Lord.

THE SACRED HEART OF JESUS

PSALM 23

    I will dwell in the house of the Lord for ever.
All **I will dwell in the house of the Lord for ever.**

    The Lord is my shepherd;
    therefore can I lack nothing.
    He makes me lie down in green pastures
    and leads me beside still waters.
All **I will dwell in the house of the Lord for ever.**

    He shall refresh my soul
    and guide me in the paths of righteousness
        for his name's sake.
    Though I walk through the valley
        of the shadow of death,
        I will fear no evil;
    for you are with me;
        your rod and your staff, they comfort me.
All **I will dwell in the house of the Lord for ever.**

    You spread a table before me
        in the presence of those who trouble me;
    you have anointed my head with oil
        and my cup shall be full.
    Surely goodness and loving mercy shall follow me
        all the days of my life,
    and I will dwell in the house of the Lord for ever.
All **I will dwell in the house of the Lord for ever.**

READING   *Romans 5.5b–11*

A reading from the Letter of Paul to the Romans.

> God's love has been poured into our hearts through the Holy Spirit that has been given to us.
> For while we were still weak, at the right time Christ died for the ungodly. Indeed, rarely will anyone die for a righteous person – though perhaps for a good person someone might actually dare to die. But God proves his love for us in that while we still were sinners Christ died for us. Much more surely then, now that we have been justified by his blood, will we be saved through him from the wrath of God. For if while we were enemies, we were reconciled to God through the death of his Son, much more surely, having been reconciled, will we be saved by his life. But more than that, we even boast in God through our Lord Jesus Christ, through whom we have now received reconciliation.

This is the word of the Lord.

ACCLAMATION

> Alleluia. **Alleluia.**
> I am the good shepherd, says the Lord:
> I know my sheep and my own know me.
> **Alleluia.**

THE SACRED HEART OF JESUS

GOSPEL *Luke 15.3–7*

Hear the Gospel of our Lord Jesus Christ according to Luke.

> Jesus told the scribes and Pharisees this parable: 'Which one of you, having a hundred sheep and losing one of them, does not leave the ninety-nine in the wilderness and go after the one that is lost until he finds it? When he has found it, he lays it on his shoulders and rejoices. And when he comes home, he calls together his friends and neighbours, saying to them, "Rejoice with me, for I have found my sheep that was lost." Just so, I tell you, there will be more joy in heaven over one sinner who repents than over ninety-nine righteous people who need no repentance.'

This is the Gospel of the Lord.

PRAYER OVER THE GIFTS

> Father of mercy and compassion,
> accept this bread and wine
>   which we offer in thanksgiving
> for the love which burns in the heart
>   of your beloved Son:
> may our offering, made one with his eternal sacrifice,
> draw us closer to you and to each other;
> we ask this in the name of the Good Shepherd,
> who laid down his life for the sheep,
> Jesus Christ our Lord.

EXTENDED PREFACE

It is indeed right and good,
our duty and our salvation,
at all times and in all places
to give you thanks and praise,
through Jesus Christ our Lord.
Lifted up on the cross,
blood and water flowed from his pierced side,
giving birth to the Church, his bride,
and foreshadowing the sacraments
which nourish us for eternal life.
Therefore earth unites with heaven
to sing a new song of praise;
we too join with all the heavenly host
evermore praising you and *saying*:

PRAYER AFTER COMMUNION

Gracious Father,
we rejoice in the gifts of love
we have received from the altar of Jesus your Son:
as he fills us with his saving presence
so enable us to transform the hearts of others
   with the life he brings,
who is alive and reigns, now and for ever.

6

Holy Baptism

In baptism we have been brought to new birth by water and the Spirit. In this votive we rejoice in the common identity and calling which unites Christian people in every time and place, and pray that all who in baptism have shared in Christ's death and resurrection may live as faithful members of his body.

*In addition to the texts provided here, material for use on the feast of the Baptism of Christ may also be used (*Common Worship: Times and Seasons, *pp. 121–37;* Common Worship: Times and Seasons, President's Edition for Holy Communion, *pp. 56–63). This votive may be used in conjunction with the corporate renewal of baptismal vows (*Common Worship: Christian Initiation, *pp. 193–6).*

The liturgical colour is white.

COLLECT

> Open the heavens, almighty Father,
> and pour out your Spirit upon your people
>   gathered in prayer.
> Renew the power of our baptismal cleansing
> and fill us with zeal for good deeds.
> Let us hear your voice once again,
> that we may recognize in your beloved Son
> the hope of everlasting life;
> through the same Jesus Christ, your Word made flesh,
> who is alive and reigns with you,
> in the unity of the Holy Spirit,
> one God, now and for ever.

READING *Titus 2.11–14, 3.4–7*

A reading from the Letter of Paul to Titus.

> The grace of God has appeared, bringing salvation to all, training us to renounce impiety and worldly passions, and in the present age to live lives that are self-controlled, upright, and godly, while we wait for the blessed hope and the manifestation of the glory of our great God and Saviour, Jesus Christ. He it is who gave himself for us that he might redeem us from all iniquity and purify for himself a people of his own who are zealous for good deeds.
>
> But when the goodness and loving-kindness of God our Saviour appeared, he saved us, not because of any works of righteousness that we had done, but according to his mercy, through the water of rebirth and renewal

by the Holy Spirit. This Spirit he poured out on us richly through Jesus Christ our Saviour, so that, having been justified by his grace, we might become heirs according to the hope of eternal life.

This is the word of the Lord.

PSALM 104.1–3, 26–27, 29–32

    Bless the Lord, O my soul.
All **Bless the Lord, O my soul.**

    O Lord my God, how excellent is your greatness!
    You are clothed with majesty and honour,
    wrapped in light as in a garment.
    You spread out the heavens like a curtain
    and lay the beams of your dwelling place
        in the waters above.
All **Bless the Lord, O my soul.**

    O Lord, how manifold are your works!
    In wisdom you have made them all;
        the earth is full of your creatures.
    There is the sea, spread far and wide,
    and there move creatures beyond number,
        both small and great.
All **Bless the Lord, O my soul.**

    All of these look to you
    to give them their food in due season.
    When you give it them, they gather it;
    you open your hand and they are filled with good.
All **Bless the Lord, O my soul.**

When you hide your face they are troubled;
when you take away their breath,
   they die and return again to the dust.
When you send forth your spirit, they are created,
and you renew the face of the earth.

All **Bless the Lord, O my soul.**

ACCLAMATION

Alleluia. **Alleluia.**
You are my Son, the Beloved:
with you I am well pleased.
Alleluia.

GOSPEL *Luke 3.15–17, 21–22*

Hear the Gospel of our Lord Jesus Christ according to Luke.

As the people were filled with expectation, and all were questioning in their hearts concerning John, whether he might be the Messiah, John answered all of them by saying, 'I baptize you with water; but one who is more powerful than I is coming; I am not worthy to untie the thong of his sandals. He will baptize you with the Holy Spirit and fire. His winnowing-fork is in his hand, to clear his threshing-floor and to gather the wheat into his granary; but the chaff he will burn with unquenchable fire.'

Now when all the people were baptized, and when Jesus also had been baptized and was praying, the heaven was opened, and the Holy Spirit descended upon him in bodily form like a dove. And a voice came from heaven, 'You are my Son, the Beloved; with you I am well pleased.'

This is the Gospel of the Lord.

PRAYER OVER THE GIFTS

Father most holy,
look upon the face of your anointed Son,
and only look on us as found him,
that the table we spread before you
   in remembrance of his passion
may be well-pleasing in your sight;
through the same Jesus Christ our Lord.

PRAYER AFTER COMMUNION

Lord of all times and peoples and nations,
in baptism you bring us to new birth
   by water and the Spirit:
may we who have shared these heavenly gifts
rejoice to be called your adopted children
and bring forth the fruit of the Spirit
   in love and joy and peace;
through Jesus Christ our Lord.

7

The Holy Eucharist

In the Eucharist Christ feeds his people with his body and blood, strengthening them for the life of discipleship. In this votive we give thanks for Christ's gift of himself in Holy Communion and pray that, as he washed the feet of his disciples on the night before he died, so we may be challenged to serve him by serving others. A votive of the Holy Eucharist is particularly appropriate on Thursdays.

In addition to the texts provided here, material for use on the feast of Corpus Christi may also be used (Common Worship: Times and Seasons, pp. 514–20; Common Worship: Times and Seasons, President's Edition for Holy Communion, pp. 292–300).

The liturgical colour is white.

THE HOLY EUCHARIST

COLLECT

> The bread you give, O God,
>   is Christ's flesh for the life of the world;
> the cup of his blood
>   is your covenant for our salvation.
> Grant that we who worship Christ in this holy mystery
> may reverence him in the needy of this world
> by lives poured for the sake of that kingdom
> where he is alive and reigns with you,
> in the unity of the Holy Spirit,
> one God, now and for ever.

READING *Proverbs 9.1–6*

A reading from the Book of Proverbs.

> Wisdom has built her house,
>   she has hewn her seven pillars.
> She has slaughtered her animals,
>   she has mixed her wine,
>   she has also set her table.
> She has sent out her servant-girls, she calls
>   from the highest places in the town,
> 'You that are simple, turn in here!'
>   To those without sense she says,
> 'Come, eat of my bread
>   and drink of the wine I have mixed.
> Lay aside immaturity, and live,
>   and walk in the way of insight.'

This is the word of the Lord.

AT ALL TIMES AND IN ALL PLACES

PSALM 111.1, 3–5, 7–10

      The Lord is ever mindful of his covenant.
All **The Lord is ever mindful of his covenant.**

      I will give thanks to the Lord with my whole heart,
      in the company of the faithful and in the congregation.
      His work is full of majesty and honour
      and his righteousness endures for ever.
All **The Lord is ever mindful of his covenant.**

      He appointed a memorial for his marvellous deeds;
      the Lord is gracious and full of compassion.
      He gave food to those who feared him;
      he is ever mindful of his covenant.
All **The Lord is ever mindful of his covenant.**

      The works of his hands are truth and justice;
      all his commandments are sure.
      They stand fast for ever and ever;
      they are done in truth and equity.
All **The Lord is ever mindful of his covenant.**

      He sent redemption to his people;
         he commanded his covenant for ever;
      holy and awesome is his name.
      The fear of the Lord is the beginning of wisdom;
         a good understanding have those who live by it;
      his praise endures for ever.
All **The Lord is ever mindful of his covenant.**

ACCLAMATION

> Alleluia. **Alleluia.**
> I am the living bread that came down from heaven:
> whoever eats of this bread will live for ever.
> **Alleluia.**

GOSPEL *Matthew 26.26–30*

Hear the Gospel of our Lord Jesus Christ according to Matthew.

> While Jesus and the twelve were eating, Jesus took a loaf of bread, and after blessing it he broke it, gave it to the disciples, and said, 'Take, eat; this is my body.' Then he took a cup, and after giving thanks he gave it to them, saying, 'Drink from it, all of you; for this is my blood of the covenant, which is poured out for many for the forgiveness of sins. I tell you, I will never again drink of this fruit of the vine until that day when I drink it new with you in my Father's kingdom.'

This is the Gospel of the Lord.

PRAYER OVER THE GIFTS

> Eternal Father,
> accept the sacrifice we offer
> for the praise and glory of your name,
> for our good and the good of all your holy Church,
> through Jesus Christ, our Great High Priest.

OR

> Faithful God,
> may the bread and wine we offer you in thanksgiving
>   for Christ's sacrifice
> bring your Church the unity and peace they signify;
> we ask this through Christ our Lord.

PRAYER AFTER COMMUNION

> Father,
> accept our thanks and praise for this sacred banquet
> in which Christ is received,
> the memory of his passion is renewed,
> our minds our filled with grace,
> and a pledge of future glory is given to us;
> to the same Lord be ascribed all worship and honour,
> now and for ever.

8

The Blessed Virgin Mary

In this votive we give thanks for Mary's life of loving obedience, and pray that we may be given grace to follow her example of bearing Christ to the world.

The Church's calendar contains a number of feasts of the Blessed Virgin Mary, celebrating her conception (8 December), birth (8 September), purification (2 February), visit to Elizabeth (31 May) and dormition / assumption (15 August). Votives of the Blessed Virgin Mary are traditionally celebrated on Saturdays and in May.

*In addition to the texts provided here, material from any of the Marian feasts and from the Common of the Blessed Virgin Mary may also be used (*Common Worship: Festivals, *pp. 268–76).*

The liturgical colour is white.

COLLECT

Faithful to your promise, O God,
you have lifted up the lowly,
clothing with heavenly splendour
the woman who bore Christ, our life and resurrection.
Grant that the Church, prefigured in Mary,
may bear Christ to the world
and come to share his triumph.
We ask this through our Lord Jesus Christ, your Son,
who is alive and reigns with you,
in the unity of the Holy Spirit,
one God, now and for ever.

READING *Galatians 4.4–7*

A reading from the Letter of Paul to the Galatians.

When the fullness of time had come, God sent his Son, born of a woman, born under the law, in order to redeem those who were under the law, so that we might receive adoption as children. And because you are children, God has sent the Spirit of his Son into our hearts, crying, 'Abba! Father!' So you are no longer a slave but a child, and if a child then also an heir, through God.

This is the word of the Lord.

THE BLESSED VIRGIN MARY

PSALM 132.12–17

    Of the fruit of your body shall I set upon your throne.
All **Of the fruit of your body shall I set upon your throne.**

    'If your children keep my covenant
       and my testimonies that I shall teach them,
    their children also shall sit upon your throne
       for evermore.'
All **Of the fruit of your body shall I set upon your throne.**

    For the Lord has chosen Zion for himself;
    he has desired her for his habitation:
    'This shall be my resting place for ever;
    here will I dwell, for I have longed for her.'
All **Of the fruit of your body shall I set upon your throne.**

    'I will abundantly bless her provision;
    her poor will I satisfy with bread.
    I will clothe her priests with salvation,
    and her faithful ones shall rejoice and sing.'
All **Of the fruit of your body shall I set upon your throne.**

ACCLAMATION

> Alleluia. **Alleluia.**
> Hail Mary, full of grace, the Lord is with you:
> blessed are you among women,
> > and blessed is the fruit of your womb.
> **Alleluia.**

GOSPEL *Luke 1.39–47*

Hear the Gospel of our Lord Jesus Christ according to Luke.

> Mary set out and went with haste to a Judean town in the hill country, where she entered the house of Zechariah and greeted Elizabeth. When Elizabeth heard Mary's greeting, the child leapt in her womb. And Elizabeth was filled with the Holy Spirit and exclaimed with a loud cry, 'Blessed are you among women, and blessed is the fruit of your womb. And why has this happened to me, that the mother of my Lord comes to me? For as soon as I heard the sound of your greeting, the child in my womb leapt for joy. And blessed is she who believed that there would be a fulfilment of what was spoken to her by the Lord.'
> And Mary said,
> > 'My soul magnifies the Lord,
> > and my spirit rejoices in God my Saviour.'

This is the Gospel of the Lord.

THE BLESSED VIRGIN MARY

PRAYER OVER THE GIFTS

> Heavenly Father,
> as you accepted the joyful obedience of Mary,
> receive the gifts we bring before you
> > with thankful hearts:
> may this great sacrament of our redemption
> > deepen our love for you
> and direct our steps as we seek to follow Mary's Son,
> Jesus Christ our Lord.

PRAYER AFTER COMMUNION

> God of boundless love,
> we give thanks for this feast which we have shared
> with Blessed Mary and the whole company of heaven:
> filled with your life-giving Spirit,
> may we with her ever magnify your holy name
> and rejoice in your salvation;
> through Jesus Christ our Lord.

9

Our Lady of Walsingham

The village of Little Walsingham in Norfolk has been a place of pilgrimage since the eleventh century, when Richeldis de Faverches, a Saxon noblewoman, received a vision in which Mary showed her the house in Nazareth in which Gabriel announced the birth of Jesus and instructed her to build a replica in Walsingham.

This Eucharist may be offered in thanksgiving and intercession for the work of the Shrine, in preparation for a pilgrimage, by those who belong to a local Walsingham cell, or on the feast of Our Lady of Walsingham (24 September). The Shrine also publishes its own booklet of Masses of the Holy House of Our Lady of Walsingham.

*In addition to the texts provided here, material for the feast of the Annunciation may also be used (*Common Worship: Festivals, *pp. 52–6;* Common Worship: Times and Seasons, President's Edition for Holy Communion, *pp. 152–8).*

The liturgical colour is white.

OUR LADY OF WALSINGHAM

COLLECT

> Almighty Father of our Lord Jesus Christ,
> you have revealed the beauty of your power
> by exalting the lowly virgin of Nazareth
> and making her the mother of our Saviour:
> may the prayers of Our Lady of Walsingham
> bring Jesus to the waiting world
> and fill the hearts of all your people
> with the presence of her child;
> who is alive and reigns with you,
> in the unity of the Holy Spirit,
> one God, now and for ever.

READING *Isaiah 7.10–14*

A reading from the prophecy of Isaiah.

> The LORD spoke to Ahaz, saying, Ask a sign of the LORD your God; let it be deep as Sheol or high as heaven. But Ahaz said, I will not ask, and I will not put the LORD to the test. Then Isaiah said: 'Hear then, O house of David! Is it too little for you to weary mortals, that you weary my God also? Therefore the Lord himself will give you a sign. Look, the young woman is with child and shall bear a son, and shall name him Immanuel.'

This is the word of the Lord.

AT ALL TIMES AND IN ALL PLACES

PSALM 146.1–2, 4–10a

    The Lord shall reign for ever.
All **The Lord shall reign for ever.**

    Praise the Lord, O my soul:
        while I live will I praise the Lord;
    as long as I have any being,
        I will sing praises to my God.
    Put not your trust in princes,
        nor in any human power,
    for there is no help in them.
All **The Lord shall reign for ever.**

    Happy are those who have the God of Jacob
        for their help,
    whose hope is in the Lord their God;
    Who made heaven and earth,
        the sea and all that is in them;
    who keeps his promise for ever.
All **The Lord shall reign for ever.**

    Who gives justice to those that suffer wrong
    and bread to those who hunger.
    The Lord looses those that are bound;
    the Lord opens the eyes of the blind.
All **The Lord shall reign for ever.**

    The Lord lifts up those who are bowed down;
    the Lord loves the righteous;
    The Lord watches over the stranger in the land;
        he upholds the orphan and widow;
    but the way of the wicked he turns upside down.
All **The Lord shall reign for ever.**

ACCLAMATION

> Alleluia. **Alleluia.**
> Here am I, the servant of the Lord:
> let it be with me according to your word.
> **Alleluia.**

GOSPEL *Luke 1.26–38*

Hear the Gospel of our Lord Jesus Christ according to Luke.

> In the sixth month the angel Gabriel was sent by God to a town in Galilee called Nazareth, to a virgin engaged to a man whose name was Joseph, of the house of David. The virgin's name was Mary. And he came to her and said, 'Greetings, favoured one! The Lord is with you.' But she was much perplexed by his words and pondered what sort of greeting this might be. The angel said to her, 'Do not be afraid, Mary, for you have found favour with God. And now, you will conceive in your womb and bear a son, and you will name him Jesus. He will be great, and will be called the Son of the Most High, and the Lord God will give to him the throne of his ancestor David. He will reign over the house of Jacob for ever, and of his kingdom there will be no end.' Mary said to the angel, 'How can this be, since I am a virgin?' The angel said to her, 'The Holy Spirit will come upon you, and the power of the Most High will overshadow you; therefore the child to be born will be holy; he will be called Son of God. And now, your relative Elizabeth in her old age has also conceived a son; and this is the sixth

month for her who was said to be barren. For nothing will be impossible with God.' Then Mary said, 'Here am I, the servant of the Lord; let it be with me according to your word.' Then the angel departed from her.

This is the Gospel of the Lord.

PRAYER OVER THE GIFTS

Eternal Father,
as your Spirit overshadowed Mary
   when she conceived the Christ,
so sanctify these gifts which we offer on your altar,
that through our communion with your incarnate Son
our lives may become a sacrifice acceptable to you;
through Jesus Christ our Lord.

PRAYER AFTER COMMUNION

Heavenly Father,
who chose the Blessed Virgin Mary
to be the mother of the promised saviour:
fill us your servants with your grace,
that in all things we may embrace your holy will
and with her rejoice in your salvation;
through Jesus Christ our Lord.

10

All Saints

The celebration of the lives of the saints is an important part of the Church's life. This Eucharist is offered in thanksgiving for all God's saints, and in intercession for all who seek to follow their example of sacrificial living in the service of Christ.

In addition to the texts provided here, material for the period from All Saints' Day to Advent may also be used (Common Worship: Times and Seasons, pp. 538–47; Common Worship: Times and Seasons, President's Edition for Holy Communion, pp. 322–9).

The liturgical colour is white.

COLLECT

God most high,
whose glory is revealed in the lives of your saints:
inspire us by their example
and assist us by their prayers,
that we may run with perseverance
   the race that is set before us,
looking to Jesus, the pioneer and perfecter of our faith,
who is alive and reigns with you,
in the unity of the Holy Spirit,
one God, now and for ever.

READING   *2 Esdras 2.42–end*

A reading from the Second Book of Esdras.

I, Ezra, saw on Mount Zion a great multitude that I could not number, and they all were praising the Lord with songs. In their midst was a young man of great stature, taller than any of the others, and on the head of each of them he placed a crown, but he was more exalted than they. And I was held spellbound. Then I asked an angel, 'Who are these, my lord?' He answered and said to me, 'These are they who have put off mortal clothing and have put on the immortal, and have confessed the name of God. Now they are being crowned, and receive palms.' Then I said to the angel, 'Who is that young man who is placing crowns on them and putting palms in their hands?' He answered and said to me, 'He is the Son of God, whom they confessed in the world.' So I began to praise those who had stood valiantly for the name of the Lord. Then the angel said to me, 'Go, tell my people how great and how many are the wonders of the Lord God that you have seen.'

This is the word of the Lord.

PSALM 34.1–2, 4–5, 9–10

    Taste and see that the Lord is gracious.
All **Taste and see that the Lord is gracious.**

    I will bless the Lord at all times;
    his praise shall ever be in my mouth.
    My soul shall glory in the Lord;
    let the humble hear and be glad.
All **Taste and see that the Lord is gracious.**

    I sought the Lord and he answered me
    and delivered me from all my fears.
    Look upon him and be radiant
    and your faces shall not be ashamed.
All **Taste and see that the Lord is gracious.**

    Fear the Lord, all you his holy ones,
    for those who fear him lack nothing.
    Lions may lack and suffer hunger,
    but those who seek the Lord
        lack nothing that is good.
All **Taste and see that the Lord is gracious.**

ACCLAMATION

> Alleluia. **Alleluia.**
> You are a chosen race, God's own people:
> called out of darkness into his marvellous light.
> **Alleluia.**

GOSPEL *Luke 6.20–23*

Hear the Gospel of our Lord Jesus Christ according to Luke.

> Jesus looked up at his disciples and said:
> 'Blessed are you who are poor,
> for yours is the kingdom of God.
> 'Blessed are you who are hungry now,
> for you will be filled.
> 'Blessed are you who weep now,
> for you will laugh.
> 'Blessed are you when people hate you, and when they exclude you, revile you, and defame you on account of the Son of Man. Rejoice on that day and leap for joy, for surely your reward is great in heaven; for that is what their ancestors did to the prophets.'

This is the Gospel of the Lord.

ALL SAINTS

PRAYER OVER THE GIFTS

Holy Father,
as the saints offer their lives
   for the sake of the kingdom,
receive the bread and wine we offer you in sacrifice;
strengthen our resolve to serve you,
that our pilgrimage of faith may lead
   to the life of eternity.
We ask this through Christ our Lord.

PRAYER AFTER COMMUNION

God, the source of holiness
   and giver of all good things:
may we who have shared at this table
as strangers and pilgrims here on earth
be welcomed with all your saints
to the heavenly feast on the day of your kingdom;
through Jesus Christ our Lord.

11

The Holy Angels

God's angels are his messengers who, as well as offering unceasing worship before the throne of heaven, are also sent to help and protect God's people on earth. As we offer this Eucharist in communion with all the heavenly host, we pray for grace to live our lives as heralds of the good news of God's kingdom.

*In addition to the texts provided here, material for the feast of St Michael and All Angels may also be used (*Common Worship: Festivals, *pp. 109–15).*

The liturgical colour is white.

THE HOLY ANGELS

COLLECT

> Everlasting God,
> you have ordained and constituted
> the ministries of angels and mortals
>   in a wonderful order:
> grant that as your holy angels
>   always serve you in heaven,
> so, at your command,
> they may help and defend us on earth;
> through Jesus Christ your Son our Lord,
> who is alive and reigns with you,
> in the unity of the Holy Spirit,
> one God, now and for ever.

READING *Tobit 12.15–end*

A reading from the Book of Tobit.

> Raphael said to Tobias and Sarah, 'I am Raphael, one of the seven angels who stand ready to enter before the glory of the Lord.'
> The two of them were shaken; they fell face down, for they were afraid. But he said to them, 'Do not be afraid; peace be with you. Bless God for evermore. As for me, when I was with you, I was not acting on my own will, but by the will of God. Bless him each and every day; sing his praises. Although you were watching me, I really did not eat or drink anything – but what you saw was a vision. So now get up from the ground, and acknowledge God. See, I am ascending to him

who sent me. Write down all these things that have happened to you.' And he ascended. Then they stood up, and could see him no more. They kept blessing God and singing his praises, and they acknowledged God for these marvellous deeds of his, when an angel of God had appeared to them.

This is the word of the Lord.

PSALM 91.1–6, 10–11

Give your angels charge over us, O God.
All **Give your angels charge over us, O God.**

Whoever dwells in the shelter of the Most High
and abides under the shadow of the Almighty,
Shall say to the Lord, 'My refuge and my stronghold,
my God, in whom I put my trust.'
All **Give your angels charge over us, O God.**

For he shall deliver you from the snare of the fowler
and from the deadly pestilence.
He shall cover you with his wings
   and you shall be safe under his feathers;
his faithfulness shall be your shield and buckler.
All **Give your angels charge over us, O God.**

You shall not be afraid of any terror by night,
nor of the arrow that flies by day;
Of the pestilence that stalks in darkness,
nor of the sickness that destroys at noonday.
All **Give your angels charge over us, O God.**

There shall no evil happen to you,
neither shall any plague come near your tent.
For he shall give his angels charge over you,
to keep you in all your ways.
All **Give your angels charge over us, O God.**

ACCLAMATION

Alleluia. **Alleluia.**
Bless the Lord you angels of the Lord:
sing his praise and exalt him for ever.
Alleluia.

GOSPEL *Luke 1.8–19*

Hear the Gospel of our Lord Jesus Christ according to Luke.

Once when Zechariah was serving as priest before God and his section was on duty, he was chosen by lot, according to the custom of the priesthood, to enter the sanctuary of the Lord and offer incense. Now at the time of the incense-offering, the whole assembly of the people was praying outside. Then there appeared to him an angel of the Lord, standing at the right side of the altar of incense. When Zechariah saw him, he was terrified; and fear overwhelmed him. But the angel said to him, 'Do not be afraid, Zechariah, for your prayer has been heard. Your wife Elizabeth will bear you a son, and you will name him John. You will have joy and gladness, and many will rejoice at his birth, for he will be great in the sight of the Lord. He must never drink wine or strong drink; even before his birth he will be filled with the Holy Spirit. He will turn many of the people of Israel to the Lord their God. With the spirit and power of Elijah he will go before him, to turn the hearts of parents to their children, and the disobedient to the wisdom of the righteous, to make ready a people prepared for the Lord.' Zechariah said to the angel, 'How will I know that this is so? For I am an old man, and my wife is getting on in years.' The angel replied, 'I am Gabriel. I stand in the presence of God, and I have been sent to speak to you and to bring you this good news.'

This is the Gospel of the Lord.

PRAYER OVER THE GIFTS

> Father,
> may your holy angels take these offerings
>   to your altar in heaven:
> then, as we receive from this altar
>   the body and blood of your Son,
> fill us with every grace and blessing;
> we ask this in the name of Jesus the Lord.

THE HOLY ANGELS

PRAYER AFTER COMMUNION

Lord of heaven,
in this Eucharist you have brought us near
   to an innumerable company of angels
   and to the spirits of the saints made perfect:
as in this food of our earthly pilgrimage
   we have shared their fellowship,
so may we come to share their joy in heaven;
through Jesus Christ our Lord.

12

Christian Unity

On the night before he died Jesus prayed that his disciples might be one, as he is one with the Father. At this Eucharist we acknowledge the sins that separate Christians from one another, and commit ourselves to work for that unity which is Christ's will and gift for the Church.

*In addition to the texts provided here, material on the theme of Christian Unity is also appropriate (*Common Worship: Times and Seasons, *pp. 138–48;* Common Worship: Festivals, *pp. 347–52).*

The liturgical colour is of the season.

CHRISTIAN UNITY

COLLECT

> Father of all,
> in baptism you anoint us with the Holy Spirit
> and make us members of Christ's body, the Church:
> help us to lead a life worthy of our calling
> that in love and humility
> we may overcome our divisions
> and reveal to the world
> > the peace and unity of your kingdom;
> through Jesus Christ your Son our Lord,
> who is alive and reigns with you,
> in the unity of the Holy Spirit,
> one God, now and for ever.

READING *Ephesians 4.1–6*

A reading from the Letter of Paul to the Ephesians.

> I, the prisoner in the Lord, beg you to lead a life worthy of the calling to which you have been called, with all humility and gentleness, with patience, bearing with one another in love, making every effort to maintain the unity of the Spirit in the bond of peace. There is one body and one Spirit, just as you were called to the one hope of your calling, one Lord, one faith, one baptism, one God and Father of all, who is above all and through all and in all.

This is the word of the Lord.

AT ALL TIMES AND IN ALL PLACES

PSALM 100

      We are God's people and the sheep of his pasture.
All **We are God's people and the sheep of his pasture.**

      O be joyful in the Lord, all the earth;
      serve the Lord with gladness
         and come before his presence with a song.
All **We are God's people and the sheep of his pasture.**

      Know that the Lord is God;
      it is he that has made us and we are his;
         we are his people and the sheep of his pasture.
All **We are God's people and the sheep of his pasture.**

      Enter his gates with thanksgiving,
         and his courts with praise;
      give thanks to him and bless his name.
All **We are God's people and the sheep of his pasture.**

      For the Lord is gracious;
         his steadfast love is everlasting;
      and his faithfulness endures
         from generation to generation.
All **We are God's people and the sheep of his pasture.**

ACCLAMATION

Alleluia. **Alleluia.**
May they all be one:
as you, Father, are in me and I am in you.
Alleluia.

GOSPEL *John 17.20–end*

Hear the Gospel of our Lord Jesus Christ according to John.

> Jesus raised his eyes to heaven and said, 'I ask not only on behalf of these, but also on behalf of those who will believe in me through their word, that they may all be one. As you, Father, are in me and I am in you, may they also be in us, so that the world may believe that you have sent me. The glory that you have given me I have given them, so that they may be one, as we are one, I in them and you in me, that they may become completely one, so that the world may know that you have sent me and have loved them even as you have loved me. Father, I desire that those also, whom you have given me, may be with me where I am, to see my glory, which you have given me because you loved me before the foundation of the world.
>
> 'Righteous Father, the world does not know you, but I know you; and these know that you have sent me. I made your name known to them, and I will make it known, so that the love with which you have loved me may be in them, and I in them.'

This is the Gospel of the Lord.

PRAYER OVER THE GIFTS

> Faithful God,
> hear our prayer for the unity of your Church:
> may this sacrament of our redemption
> strengthen the bonds of love and peace
> which unite us to you
>   and all who confess the name of Jesus,
> who is Lord for ever and ever.

PRAYER AFTER COMMUNION

> Eternal God and Father,
> whose Son at supper prayed that his disciples
>   might be one,
> as he is one with you;
> draw us closer to him,
> that in common love and obedience to you
> we may be united to one another
> in the fellowship of the one Spirit,
> that the world may believe that he is Lord,
> to your eternal glory;
> through Jesus Christ our Lord.

13

Mission of the Church

St Paul encourages the Christian community in Corinth to see every Eucharist as an act of mission: 'as often as you eat this bread and drink the cup, you proclaim the Lord's death until he comes' (1 Corinthians 11.26). This Eucharist is offered in thanksgiving for God's call to share in his mission for the world, and in intercession for the missionary work of the Church.

The eve of St Andrew's Day (29 November) may be observed as a day of intercession and thanksgiving for the missionary work of the Church.

In addition to the texts provided here, material on the theme of Mission is also appropriate (Common Worship: Times and Seasons, pp. 149–58; Common Worship: Festivals, pp. 342–6).

The liturgical colour is of the season.

COLLECT

God, the giver of life,
whose Holy Spirit wells up within your Church:
by the Spirit's gifts equip us to live the gospel of Christ
   and make us eager to do your will,
that we may share with the whole creation
   the joys of eternal life;
through Jesus Christ your Son our Lord,
who is alive and reigns with you
in the unity of the Holy Spirit,
one God, now and for ever.

READING   *Isaiah 52.7–10*

A reading from the prophecy of Isaiah.

How beautiful upon the mountains
   are the feet of the messenger who announces peace,
who brings good news,
   who announces salvation,
   who says to Zion, 'Your God reigns.'
Listen! Your sentinels lift up their voices,
   together they sing for joy;
for in plain sight they see
   the return of the Lord to Zion.
Break forth together into singing,
   you ruins of Jerusalem;
for the Lord has comforted his people,
   he has redeemed Jerusalem.

THE MISSION OF THE CHURCH

The Lord has bared his holy arm
   before the eyes of all the nations;
and all the ends of the earth shall see
   the salvation of our God.

This is the word of the Lord.

PSALM 47.1–4, 8, 10

Sing to the Lord with shouts of joy.
All **Sing to the Lord with shouts of joy.**

Clap your hands together, all you peoples;
O sing to God with shouts of joy.
For the Lord Most High is to be feared;
he is the great King over all the earth.
All **Sing to the Lord with shouts of joy.**

He subdued the peoples under us
and the nations under our feet.
He has chosen our heritage for us,
the pride of Jacob, whom he loves.
All **Sing to the Lord with shouts of joy.**

God reigns over the nations;
God has taken his seat upon his holy throne.
For the powers of the earth belong to God
and he is very highly exalted.
All **Sing to the Lord with shouts of joy.**

ACCLAMATION

>Alleluia. **Alleluia.**
>Let your light so shine before others:
>that they may see your good works and give glory to
> your Father in heaven.
>**Alleluia.**

GOSPEL *Matthew 5.13–16*

Hear the Gospel of our Lord Jesus Christ according to Matthew.

>Jesus said to the crowds: 'You are the salt of the earth; but if salt has lost its taste, how can its saltiness be restored? It is no longer good for anything, but is thrown out and trampled underfoot.
> 'You are the light of the world. A city built on a hill cannot be hidden. No one after lighting a lamp puts it under the bushel basket, but on the lampstand, and it gives light to all in the house. In the same way, let your light shine before others, so that they may see your good works and give glory to your Father in heaven.'

This is the Gospel of the Lord.

PRAYER OVER THE GIFTS

> Father,
> when we eat this bread and drink this cup
> we proclaim Christ's death until he comes:
> as we offer his saving sacrifice,
> make us one with him in his mission for the world;
> we ask this for his name's sake.

PRAYER AFTER COMMUNION

> Lord of all nations,
> sanctify and unite us by the Eucharist
>   we have celebrated:
> through the living witness of your Church
> may the Gospel of Christ be proclaimed in every place,
> that all peoples may know him as Lord and King,
> who is alive and reigns, now and for ever.

14

Vocations

The Bible contains many accounts of individuals responding to God's call. In this Eucharist we give thanks for God's call to all the baptized, and pray for an increase in vocations to the ordained ministry of the Church.

Ember Days (which may be observed, at the direction of the Bishop, in the week before an ordination or on the Wednesdays, Fridays and Saturdays within the weeks before the Third Sunday of Advent, the Second Sunday of Lent and the Sundays nearest to 29 June and 29 September) are an appropriate time for intercession for vocations, as is the week following Vocations Sunday (the Fourth Sunday of Easter).

In addition to the texts provided here, material for use on Ember Days is also appropriate (Common Worship: Times and Seasons, pp. 636–42; Common Worship: Festivals, pp. 357–63).

The liturgical colour is of the season.

COLLECT

God most holy,
in baptism you call us to witness to your love
and work for the coming of your kingdom:
inspire the hearts of all Christian people
to discern your call in their lives,
and raise up worthy ministers
to serve as deacons, priests and bishops in your Church;
through Jesus Christ your Son our Lord,
who is alive and reigns with you,
in the unity of the Holy Spirit,
one God, now and for ever.

READING *Jeremiah 1.4–10*

A reading from the prophecy of Jeremiah.

The word of the LORD came to me saying,
  'Before I formed you in the womb I knew you,
  and before you were born I consecrated you;
  I appointed you a prophet to the nations.'
Then I said, 'Ah, Lord GOD! Truly I do not know how
to speak, for I am only a boy.' But the LORD said to me,
  'Do not say, "I am only a boy";
  for you shall go to all to whom I send you,
  and you shall speak whatever I command you.
  Do not be afraid of them,
  for I am with you to deliver you,
            says the LORD.'
Then the LORD put out his hand and touched my mouth;

and the LORD said to me,
> 'Now I have put my words in your mouth.
> See, today I appoint you over nations and over
>   kingdoms,
> to pluck up and to pull down,
> to destroy and to overthrow,
> to build and to plant.'

This is the word of the Lord.

PSALM 84.1, 3–4, 11

> Blessed are those who put their trust in the Lord.

All **Blessed are those who put their trust in the Lord.**

> How lovely is your dwelling place, O Lord of hosts!
> My soul has a desire and longing
>   to enter the courts of the Lord;
>   my heart and my flesh rejoice in the living God.

All **Blessed are those who put their trust in the Lord.**

> Blessed are they who dwell in your house:
> they will always be praising you.
> Blessed are those whose strength is in you,
> in whose heart are the highways to Zion.

All **Blessed are those who put their trust in the Lord.**

> For the Lord God is both sun and shield;
>   he will give grace and glory;
> no good thing shall the Lord withhold
>   from those who walk with integrity.

All **Blessed are those who put their trust in the Lord.**

ACCLAMATION

Alleluia. **Alleluia.**
You did not choose me but I chose you:
and I appointed you to go and bear fruit,
   fruit that will last.
Alleluia.

GOSPEL *John 4.31–38*

Hear the Gospel of our Lord Jesus Christ according to John.

> The disciples were urging Jesus, 'Rabbi, eat something.' But he said to them, 'I have food to eat that you do not know about.' So the disciples said to one another, 'Surely no one has brought him something to eat?' Jesus said to them, 'My food is to do the will of him who sent me and to complete his work. Do you not say, "Four months more, then comes the harvest"? But I tell you, look around you, and see how the fields are ripe for harvesting. The reaper is already receiving wages and is gathering fruit for eternal life, so that sower and reaper may rejoice together. For here the saying holds true, "One sows and another reaps." I sent you to reap that for which you did not labour. Others have laboured, and you have entered into their labour.'

This is the Gospel of the Lord.

PRAYER OVER THE GIFTS

Father,
with these gifts of bread and wine
we celebrate the redeeming sacrifice of Jesus Christ:
open our hearts to respond to his call
and accept our lives as an offering in his sight;
who is our Great High Priest, now and for ever.

PRAYER AFTER COMMUNION

Lord of the harvest,
you have fed your people in this sacrament
with the fruits of creation made holy by your Spirit:
by your grace raise up among us faithful labourers
to sow your word and reap the harvest of souls;
through Jesus Christ our Lord.

PART TWO

The Global and Local Community

15

The Environment

In this votive we give thanks for God's gift of creation and pray for those involved in making decisions which affect the environment, and for all people of faith, that we may be responsible stewards of the resources of the earth.

In addition to the texts provided here, appropriate material for the Seasons and Festivals of the Agricultural Year may be used (Common Worship: Times and Seasons, pp. 596–633; Common Worship: Times and Seasons, President's Edition for Holy Communion, pp. 322–9).

The liturgical colour is of the season.

AT ALL TIMES AND IN ALL PLACES

COLLECT

>Loving Father,
>in your work of creation you blessed the earth
>>and made us your stewards:
>teach us to respect the environment as your gift,
>to conserve its resources,
>and preserve it for future generations,
>that they may also praise you for your goodness;
>through Jesus Christ your Son our Lord,
>who is alive and reigns with you,
>in the unity of the Holy Spirit,
>one God, now and for ever.

READING   *Deuteronomy 8.7–18*

A reading from the Book of Deuteronomy.

>Moses said to all Israel: 'The LORD your God is bringing you into a good land, a land with flowing streams, with springs and underground waters welling up in valleys and hills, a land of wheat and barley, of vines and fig trees and pomegranates, a land of olive trees and honey, a land where you may eat bread without scarcity, where you will lack nothing, a land whose stones are iron and from whose hills you may mine copper. You shall eat your fill and bless the LORD your God for the good land that he has given you.
>'Take care that you do not forget the LORD your God, by failing to keep his commandments, his ordinances, and his statutes, which I am commanding you today.

THE ENVIRONMENT

When you have eaten your fill and have built fine houses and live in them, and when your herds and flocks have multiplied, and your silver and gold is multiplied, and all that you have is multiplied, then do not exalt yourself, forgetting the LORD your God, who brought you out of the land of Egypt, out of the house of slavery, who led you through the great and terrible wilderness, an arid waste-land with poisonous snakes and scorpions. He made water flow for you from flint rock, and fed you in the wilderness with manna that your ancestors did not know, to humble you and to test you, and in the end to do you good. Do not say to yourself, "My power and the might of my own hand have gained me this wealth." But remember the LORD your God, for it is he who gives you power to get wealth, so that he may confirm his covenant that he swore to your ancestors, as he is doing today.'

This is the word of the Lord.

PSALM 148.1–6

    Let all creation praise the Lord.
All **Let all creation praise the Lord.**

    Praise the Lord from the heavens;
    praise him in the heights.
    Praise him, all you his angels;
    praise him, all his host.
All **Let all creation praise the Lord.**

Praise him, sun and moon;
praise him, all you stars of light.
Praise him, heaven of heavens,
and you waters above the heavens.

All **Let all creation praise the Lord.**

Let them praise the name of the Lord,
for he commanded and they were created.
He made them fast for ever and ever;
he gave them a law which shall not pass away.

All **Let all creation praise the Lord.**

ACCLAMATION

Alleluia. **Alleluia.**
The Lord will give all that is good:
and our land will yield its increase.
Alleluia.

GOSPEL   *Matthew 7.24–27*

Hear the Gospel of our Lord Jesus Christ according to Matthew.

Jesus said to the crowds: 'Everyone who hears these words of mine and acts on them will be like a wise man who built his house on rock. The rain fell, the floods came, and the winds blew and beat on that house, but it did not fall, because it had been founded on rock. And everyone who hears these words of mine and does not act on them will be like a foolish man who built his house on sand. The rain fell, and the floods came, and the winds blew and beat against that house, and it fell – and great was its fall!'

This is the Gospel of the Lord.

PRAYER OVER THE GIFTS

> Faithful God,
> from your abundant generosity
> > we offer you these gifts.
>
> May this Eucharist
> open our eyes to your presence in the world,
> satisfy our hunger with the bread of life,
> and lead us all to the heavenly banquet;
> through Jesus Christ our Lord.

PRAYER AFTER COMMUNION

> Lord of the harvest,
> with joy we have offered thanksgiving
> > for your love in creation
>
> and have shared the bread and the wine of the kingdom:
> by your grace plant within us a reverence
> > for all that you give us
>
> and make us generous and wise stewards
> > of the good things we enjoy;
>
> through Jesus Christ our Lord.

16

The Peace of the World

When Christians gather for worship, the peace we share with each other is Christ's gift to us, the same peace he shared with his apostles after the resurrection. At this Eucharist, we acknowledge the ways our words and actions lead to strife and discord, and pray for peace within and between peoples, nations and communities.

In addition to the texts provided here, material from Common Worship: Festivals, *pp. 353–7, is also appropriate.*

The liturgical colour is of the season.

THE PEACE OF THE WORLD

COLLECT

> Father of all,
> your risen Son gave new hope to his apostles
>   with words of peace
>   and the assurance of his presence:
> send your Holy Spirit into the troubled places
>   of the world,
> bless them with Christ's gift of peace,
> and strengthen the resolve of all who work
>   to reveal your kingdom on earth as in heaven;
> through Jesus Christ your Son our Lord,
> who is alive and reigns with you,
> in the unity of the Holy Spirit,
> one God, now and for ever.

READING *James 3.13–end*

A reading from the Letter of James.

> Who is wise and understanding among you? Show by your good life that your works are done with gentleness born of wisdom. But if you have bitter envy and selfish ambition in your hearts, do not be boastful and false to the truth. Such wisdom does not come down from above, but is earthly, unspiritual, devilish. For where there is envy and selfish ambition, there will also be disorder and wickedness of every kind. But the wisdom from above is first pure, then peaceable, gentle, willing to yield, full of mercy and good fruits, without a trace of

partiality or hypocrisy. And a harvest of righteousness
is sown in peace for those who make peace.

This is the word of the Lord.

PSALM 72.1–8

    Give your people the blessing of peace.
All **Give your people the blessing of peace.**

    Give the king your judgements, O God,
    and your righteousness to the son of a king.
    Then shall he judge your people righteously
    and your poor with justice.
All **Give your people the blessing of peace.**

    May the mountains bring forth peace,
    and the little hills righteousness for the people.
    May he defend the poor among the people,
    deliver the children of the needy
        and crush the oppressor.
All **Give your people the blessing of peace.**

    May he live as long as the sun and moon endure,
    from one generation to another.
    May he come down like the rain upon the mown grass,
    like the showers that water the earth.
All **Give your people the blessing of peace.**

THE PEACE OF THE WORLD

In his time shall righteousness flourish;
and abundance of peace
   till the moon shall be no more.
May his dominion extend from sea to sea,
and from the River to the ends of the earth.

All **Give your people the blessing of peace.**

ACCLAMATION

Alleluia. **Alleluia.**
Blessed are the peacemakers:
for they shall be called children of God.
Alleluia.

GOSPEL *John 20.19–21*

Hear the Gospel of our Lord Jesus Christ according to John.

When it was evening on that day, the first day of the week, and the doors of the house where the disciples had met were locked for fear of the Jews, Jesus came and stood among them and said, 'Peace be with you.' After he said this, he showed them his hands and his side. Then the disciples rejoiced when they saw the Lord. Jesus said to them again, 'Peace be with you. As the Father has sent me, so I send you.'

This is the Gospel of the Lord.

AT ALL TIMES AND IN ALL PLACES

PRAYER OVER THE GIFTS

> Father of mercy,
> your Son has reconciled us to one another and to you:
> through these gifts of bread and wine
> help us to experience the salvation he won for us
>   and the peace of the kingdom,
> where he is Lord, for ever and ever.

PRAYER AFTER COMMUNION

> God our Father,
> your Son is our peace
> and his cross the sign of reconciliation:
> help us, who share the broken bread,
> to bring together what is scattered
> and to bind up what is wounded,
> that Christ may bring in the everlasting kingdom
>   of his peace;
> who is alive and reigns, now and for ever.

17

The Global Community (One World)

God's call to justice is an important theme within the teaching of the Old Testament prophets, and is embodied in the ministry of Christ. This Eucharist is offered for those who suffer as a result of any kind of injustice, and for all peoples and nations, that they may strive to imitate the justice of God. It may be used during 'One World Week', which is observed each year in October, and encourages people of different faiths and traditions to focus on the issue of global justice.

In addition to the texts provided here, material from Common Worship: Festivals, *pp. 364–5, is also appropriate.*

The liturgical colour is of the season.

COLLECT

> Almighty God,
> you have entrusted this earth to us,
> and have called us to be citizens of heaven:
> grant us such shame and repentance for the disorder,
>   injustice and cruelty
> which are among us,
> that fleeing to you for pardon and for grace
> we may henceforth set ourselves to establish that city
> which has justice for its foundation and love for its law,
> whereof you are the architect and maker;
> through Jesus Christ your Son our Lord,
> who is alive and reigns with you,
> in the unity of the Holy Spirit,
> one God, now and for ever.

READING   *Amos 5.4a, 11–15*

A reading from the prophecy of Amos.

> Thus says the LORD to the house of Israel:
> Because you trample on the poor
>   and take from them levies of grain,
> you have built houses of hewn stone,
>   but you shall not live in them;
> you have planted pleasant vineyards,
>   but you shall not drink their wine.
> For I know how many are your transgressions,
>   and how great are your sins –

THE GLOBAL COMMUNITY (ONE WORLD)

you who afflict the righteous, who take a bribe,
   and push aside the needy in the gate.
Therefore the prudent will keep silent in such a time;
   for it is an evil time.

Seek good and not evil,
   that you may live;
and so the LORD, the God of hosts, will be with you,
   just as you have said.
Hate evil and love good,
   and establish justice in the gate;
it may be that the LORD, the God of hosts,
   will be gracious to the remnant of Joseph.

This is the word of the Lord.

PSALM 12.1–7

Rise up to help us, O Lord our God.
All **Rise up to help us, O Lord our God.**

Help me, Lord, for no one godly is left;
   the faithful have vanished from the whole human race.
They all speak falsely with their neighbour;
they flatter with their lips,
   but speak from a double heart.
All **Rise up to help us, O Lord our God.**

O that the Lord would cut off all flattering lips
   and the tongue that speaks proud boasts!
Those who say, 'With our tongue will we prevail;
   our lips we will use; who is lord over us?'
All **Rise up to help us, O Lord our God.**

'Because of the oppression of the needy,
   and the groaning of the poor;
I will rise up now', says the Lord,
   'and set them in the safety that they long for.'

All **Rise up to help us, O Lord our God.**

The words of the Lord are pure words,
like silver refined in the furnace
   and purified seven times in the fire.
You, O Lord, will watch over us
and guard us from this generation for ever.

All **Rise up to help us, O Lord our God.**

ACCLAMATION

Alleluia. **Alleluia.**
Blessed are those who hunger and thirst
   for righteousness:
for they will be filled.
Alleluia.

GOSPEL   *Luke 16.19–end*

Hear the Gospel of our Lord Jesus Christ according to Luke.

Jesus said to the disciples, 'There was a rich man who was dressed in purple and fine linen and who feasted sumptuously every day. And at his gate lay a poor man named Lazarus, covered with sores, who longed to satisfy his hunger with what fell from the rich man's table; even the dogs would come and lick his sores. The poor man died and was carried away by the angels to be with Abraham. The rich man also died and was buried. In Hades, where he was being tormented, he looked up and saw Abraham far away with Lazarus by his side. He called out, "Father Abraham, have mercy on me, and send Lazarus to dip the tip of his finger in water and cool my tongue; for I am in agony in these flames." But Abraham said, "Child, remember that during your lifetime you received your good things, and Lazarus in like manner evil things; but now he is comforted here, and you are in agony. Besides all this, between you and us a great chasm has been fixed, so that those who might want to pass from here to you cannot do so, and no one can cross from there to us." He said, "Then, father, I beg you to send him to my father's house – for I have five brothers – that he may warn them, so that they will not also come into this place of torment." Abraham replied, "They have Moses and the prophets; they should listen to them." He said, "No, father Abraham; but if someone goes to them from the dead, they will repent." He said to him, "If they do not listen to Moses and the prophets, neither will they be convinced even if someone rises from the dead."'

This is the Gospel of the Lord.

PRAYER OVER THE GIFTS

God of Abraham,
hear our prayer for justice in your world
and accept this offering as a sacrifice of righteousness:
may love and truth defeat hatred and oppression,
that all people may find true freedom as your children;
through Jesus our brother and Lord.

PRAYER AFTER COMMUNION

God of the nations,
in this Eucharist you have fed us at your table
with the fruits of redemption:
may our communion with Christ awaken in us
   a longing for justice,
that all peoples may live in harmony,
united in your love and guided by your truth.
We ask this through Christ our Lord.

18

Those in Authority

In this Eucharist we respond to St Paul's injunction to pray for all in positions of authority. We pray for the right use of power, and for all peoples, that we may imitate the example of Christ who came not to be served but to serve.

The liturgical colour is of the season.

COLLECT

>Sovereign God,
>you know the longings of human hearts
>and guide the world in wisdom and love.
>In your goodness
>watch over those in authority,
>so that peoples everywhere may enjoy
>   freedom, security and peace;
>through Jesus Christ your Son our Lord,
>who is alive and reigns with you,
>in the unity of the Holy Spirit,
>one God, now and for ever.

AT ALL TIMES AND IN ALL PLACES

READING   *1 Timothy 2.1–7*

A reading from the First Letter of Paul to Timothy.

> I, Paul, urge that supplications, prayers, intercessions, and thanksgivings be made for everyone, for kings and all who are in high positions, so that we may lead a quiet and peaceable life in all godliness and dignity. This is right and is acceptable in the sight of God our Saviour, who desires everyone to be saved and to come to the knowledge of the truth. For
> there is one God;
> > there is also one mediator between God and humankind,
> Christ Jesus, himself human,
> > who gave himself a ransom for all
> – this was attested at the right time. For this I was appointed a herald and an apostle (I am telling the truth, I am not lying), a teacher of the Gentiles in faith and truth.

This is the word of the Lord.

THOSE IN AUTHORITY

PSALM 99.1–2, 4, 6, 8

    Exalt the Lord our God, for he is holy.
All **Exalt the Lord our God, for he is holy.**

    The Lord is king: let the peoples tremble;
    he is enthroned above the cherubim:
        let the earth shake.
    The Lord is great in Zion
    and high above all peoples.
All **Exalt the Lord our God, for he is holy.**

    Mighty king, who loves justice,
        you have established equity;
    you have executed justice
        and righteousness in Jacob.
All **Exalt the Lord our God, for he is holy.**

    Moses and Aaron among his priests
        and Samuel among those who call upon his name;
    they called upon the Lord and he answered them.
All **Exalt the Lord our God, for he is holy.**

    You answered them, O Lord our God;
    you were a God who forgave them
        and pardoned them for their offences.
All **Exalt the Lord our God, for he is holy.**

ACCLAMATION

> Alleluia. **Alleluia.**
> The Son of Man came not to be served but to serve:
> and to give his life a ransom for many.
> **Alleluia.**

GOSPEL *Mark 10.42–45*

Hear the Gospel of our Lord Jesus Christ according to Mark.

> Jesus called the ten and said to them, 'You know that among the Gentiles those whom they recognize as their rulers lord it over them, and their great ones are tyrants over them. But it is not so among you; but whoever wishes to become great among you must be your servant, and whoever wishes to be first among you must be slave of all. For the Son of Man came not to be served but to serve, and to give his life a ransom for many.'

This is the Gospel of the Lord.

PRAYER OVER THE GIFTS

>Shepherd of Israel,
>through the gifts we offer on your altar
>save us from the self-seeking desire
>>for privilege and power.
>Fill our hearts with sacrificial love
>and inspire us in the service of your kingdom;
>through Jesus Christ our Lord.

PRAYER AFTER COMMUNION

>God of power and might,
>we thank you for feeding us at the table of your Son,
>to whom belongs all authority in heaven and on earth.
>Help us to support those who govern in accordance
>>with his law of love,
>and to live as his anointed servants,
>to whom be glory through every age and for ever.

19

Social Justice and Responsibility

At this Eucharist we pray that the community of the baptized may respond to God's call to defend the weak, seek justice and peace, and serve Christ in all people.

In addition to the texts provided here, material from Common Worship: Festivals, *pp. 364–5, is also appropriate.*

The liturgical colour is of the season.

COLLECT

O God, the King of righteousness,
lead us, we pray, in ways of justice and peace;
inspire us to break down all tyranny and oppression,
to gain for everyone their due reward
and from everyone their due service;
that each may live for all,
and all may care for each,
in the name of Jesus Christ our Lord,
who is alive and reigns with you,
in the unity of the Holy Spirit,
one God, now and for ever.

SOCIAL JUSTICE AND RESPONSIBILITY

READING *Amos 5.21–24*

A reading from the prophecy of Amos.

> I hate, I despise your festivals,
>   and I take no delight in your solemn assemblies.
> Even though you offer me your burnt offerings and
>   grain offerings,
>   I will not accept them;
> and the offerings of well-being of your fatted animals
>   I will not look upon.
> Take away from me the noise of your songs;
>   I will not listen to the melody of your harps.
> But let justice roll down like waters,
>   and righteousness like an ever-flowing stream.

This is the word of the Lord.

PSALM *146.4, 6–9a, 10*

> The Lord keeps his promise for ever.
All **The Lord keeps his promise for ever.**

> Happy are those who have the God of Jacob
>   for their help,
> whose hope is in the Lord their God;
> who gives justice to those that suffer wrong
> and bread to those who hunger.
All **The Lord keeps his promise for ever.**

The Lord looses those that are bound;
the Lord opens the eyes of the blind;
The Lord lifts up those who are bowed down;
the Lord loves the righteous.

All **The Lord keeps his promise for ever.**

The Lord watches over the stranger in the land;
   he upholds the orphan and widow.
The Lord shall reign for ever,
   your God, O Zion, throughout all generations.

All **The Lord keeps his promise for ever.**

ACCLAMATION

Alleluia. **Alleluia.**
Blessed are the pure in heart:
for they will see God.
Alleluia.

GOSPEL *Matthew 5.1–12*

Hear the Gospel of our Lord Jesus Christ according to Matthew.

When Jesus saw the crowds, he went up the mountain; and after he sat down, his disciples came to him. Then he began to speak, and taught them, saying:
  'Blessed are the poor in spirit, for theirs is the kingdom of heaven.

'Blessed are those who mourn, for they will be comforted.

'Blessed are the meek, for they will inherit the earth.

'Blessed are those who hunger and thirst for righteousness, for they will be filled.

'Blessed are the merciful, for they will receive mercy.

'Blessed are the pure in heart, for they will see God.

'Blessed are the peacemakers, for they will be called children of God.

'Blessed are those who are persecuted for righteousness' sake, for theirs is the kingdom of heaven.

'Blessed are you when people revile you and persecute you and utter all kinds of evil against you falsely on my account. Rejoice and be glad, for your reward is great in heaven, for in the same way they persecuted the prophets who were before you.'

This is the Gospel of the Lord.

PRAYER OVER THE GIFTS

Merciful God,
accept the gifts we set before you.
By the power of your Spirit purify our hearts,
that as we dedicate our lives in your service
we may see you face to face;
through Jesus Christ our Lord.

PRAYER AFTER COMMUNION

> Blessed God,
> help us, whom you have fed and satisfied
>   in this Eucharist,
> to hunger and thirst for what is right;
> help us, who here have rejoiced and been glad,
> to stand with those who are persecuted and reviled;
> help us, who here have glimpsed the life of heaven,
> to strive for the cause of right
> and for the coming of the kingdom of Jesus Christ,
> who is alive and reigns, now and for ever.

20

Reconciliation

Whenever the Eucharist is celebrated, God invites us, despite our unworthiness, to be transformed by the reconciling love of Christ. In this celebration, we pray that we may be given grace to share in Christ's work of reconciliation, bringing unity and hope to the world.

The Prayer after Communion, 'Father of all, we give you thanks and praise', based on the Parable of the Prodigal Son, is particularly appropriate.

The liturgical colour is of the season.

COLLECT

> Almighty God,
> who called your Church to bear witness
> that you were in Christ reconciling the world to yourself:
> help us to proclaim the good news of your love,
> that all who hear it may be drawn to you;
> through him who was lifted up on the cross,
> and reigns with you in the unity of the Holy Spirit,
> one God, now and for ever.

READING *2 Corinthians 5.16–end*

A reading from the Second Letter of Paul to the Corinthians.

> From now on we regard no one from a human point of view; even though we once knew Christ from a human point of view, we know him no longer in that way. So if anyone is in Christ, there is a new creation: everything old has passed away; see, everything has become new! All this is from God, who reconciled us to himself through Christ, and has given us the ministry of reconciliation; that is, in Christ God was reconciling the world to himself, not counting their trespasses against them, and entrusting the message of reconciliation to us. So we are ambassadors for Christ, since God is making his appeal through us; we entreat you on behalf of Christ, be reconciled to God. For our sake he made him to be sin who knew no sin, so that in him we might become the righteousness of God.

This is the word of the Lord.

PSALM *85.1–2, 4, 6, 7a, 10–11*

> Show us your mercy, O Lord.

All **Show us your mercy, O Lord.**

> Lord, you were gracious to your land,
> you restored the fortunes of Jacob.
> You forgave the offence of your people
> and covered all their sins.

All **Show us your mercy, O Lord.**

Restore us again, O God our Saviour,
and let your anger cease from us.
Will you not give us life again,
that your people may rejoice in you?
All **Show us your mercy, O Lord.**

Mercy and truth are met together,
righteousness and peace have kissed each other;
Truth shall spring up from the earth
and righteousness look down from heaven.
All **Show us your mercy, O Lord.**

ACCLAMATION

Alleluia. **Alleluia.**
This son of mine was dead and is alive again:
he was lost and is found.
Alleluia.

GOSPEL *Luke 15.11–24a*

Hear the Gospel of our Lord Jesus Christ according to Luke.

Jesus said, 'There was a man who had two sons. The younger of them said to his father, "Father, give me the share of the property that will belong to me." So he divided his property between them. A few days later the younger son gathered all he had and travelled to a distant country, and there he squandered his property in dissolute living. When he had spent everything, a severe famine took place throughout that country, and he began to be in need. So he went and hired himself out to one of the citizens of that country, who sent him to his fields to feed the pigs. He would gladly have filled himself with the pods that the pigs were eating; and no one gave him anything. But when he came to himself he said, "How many of my father's hired hands have bread enough and to spare, but here I am dying of hunger! I will get up and go to my father, and I will say to him, 'Father, I have sinned against heaven and before you; I am no longer worthy to be called your son; treat me like one of your hired hands.'" So he set off and went to his father. But while he was still far off, his father saw him and was filled with compassion; he ran and put his arms around him and kissed him. Then the son said to him, "Father, I have sinned against heaven and before you; I am no longer worthy to be called your son." But the father said to his slaves, "Quickly, bring out a robe – the best one – and put it on him; put a ring on his finger and sandals on his feet. And get the fatted calf and kill it, and let us eat and celebrate; for this son of mine was dead and is alive again; he was lost and is found!"'

This is the Gospel of the Lord.

RECONCILIATION

PRAYER OVER THE GIFTS

God of compassion,
through this sacrifice of our redemption,
grant that we who have wandered from the path of life
may find our true home in heaven.
We ask this through Christ our Lord.

PRAYER AFTER COMMUNION

Father in heaven,
we thank you for inviting us to feast
 at the table of your kingdom.
May we who have been nourished
 by Christ's body and blood
never forget our need to forgive others
 as you have forgiven us,
through Jesus Christ our Lord.

21

The Sovereign and Our National Life

Prayer for the Sovereign has an important place in the worshipping life of the churches of the United Kingdom. In this votive we pray not only for the Queen, but also for those who serve in national and local government, and for all the peoples of the United Kingdom.

In addition to the texts provided here, material from Common Worship: Festivals, *p. 367, is also appropriate.*

The liturgical colour is of the season.

THE SOVEREIGN AND OUR NATIONAL LIFE

COLLECT

> Almighty God, the fountain of all goodness,
> bless our Sovereign Lady, Queen Elizabeth,
> and all who are in authority under her;
> that they may order all things
>   in wisdom and equity, righteousness and peace,
> to the honour and glory of your name
> and the good of your Church and people;
> through Jesus Christ your Son our Lord,
> who is alive and reigns with you,
> in the unity of the Holy Spirit,
> one God, now and for ever.

READING *Proverbs 8.1–16*

A reading from the Book of Proverbs.

> Does not wisdom call,
>   and does not understanding raise her voice?
> On the heights, beside the way,
>   at the crossroads she takes her stand;
> beside the gates in front of the town,
>   at the entrance of the portals she cries out:
> 'To you, O people, I call,
>   and my cry is to all that live.
> O simple ones, learn prudence;
>   acquire intelligence, you who lack it.
> Hear, for I will speak noble things,
>   and from my lips will come what is right;
> for my mouth will utter truth;
>   wickedness is an abomination to my lips.

AT ALL TIMES AND IN ALL PLACES

All the words of my mouth are righteous;
   there is nothing twisted or crooked in them.
They are all straight to one who understands
   and right to those who find knowledge.
Take my instruction instead of silver,
   and knowledge rather than choice gold;
for wisdom is better than jewels,
   and all that you may desire cannot compare with her.
I, wisdom, live with prudence,
   and I attain knowledge and discretion.
The fear of the LORD is hatred of evil.
Pride and arrogance and the way of evil
   and perverted speech I hate.
I have good advice and sound wisdom;
   I have insight, I have strength.
By me kings reign,
   and rulers decree what is just;
by me rulers rule,
   and nobles, all who govern rightly.'

This is the word of the Lord.

PSALM 101.1–4, 9–10

   Make me wise in the way that is perfect.
All **Make me wise in the way that is perfect.**

   I will sing of faithfulness and justice;
   to you, O Lord, will I sing.
   Let me be wise in the way that is perfect:
   when will you come to me?
All **Make me wise in the way that is perfect.**

I will walk with purity of heart
within the walls of my house.
I will not set before my eyes
a counsel that is evil.

All **Make me wise in the way that is perfect.**

My eyes are upon the faithful in the land,
that they might dwell with me.
One who walks in the way that is pure
shall be my servant.

All **Make me wise in the way that is perfect.**

ACCLAMATION

Alleluia. **Alleluia.**
The kings of the Gentiles lord it over them:
but I am among you as one who serves.
Alleluia.

GOSPEL *Luke 22.24–27*

Hear the Gospel of our Lord Jesus Christ according to Luke.

A dispute also arose among the disciples as to which one of them was to be regarded as the greatest. But Jesus said to them, 'The kings of the Gentiles lord it over them; and those in authority over them are called benefactors. But not so with you; rather the greatest among you must become like the youngest, and the leader like one who serves. For who is greater, the one who is at the table or the one who serves? Is it not the one at the table? But I am among you as one who serves.'

This is the Gospel of the Lord.

PRAYER OVER THE GIFTS

> Eternal Father,
> look with love upon the offering of your Church:
> may the sacrifice of Christ our King
> inspire all who govern to follow his example
>   of selfless humility,
> who is alive and reigns, now and for ever.

PRAYER AFTER COMMUNION

> Generous God,
> may we who have been fed at your table
> reveal to the people of this nation
>   the loving service of Christ,
> who came not to be served, but to serve;
> to whom be ascribed glory and power,
>   now and in all eternity.

22

Education

At this Eucharist we rejoice that Jesus Christ is the Wisdom of God, and pray for all involved in education and learning. This votive is particularly appropriate in the days before or after Education Sunday (the Ninth Sunday before Easter), and at the beginning of the academic year.

The liturgical colour is of the season.

COLLECT

> God of truth,
> you give gifts of wisdom and insight
> to fathom the depths of your love,
> grant the help of your Spirit
>   to all involved in education
> that those who teach and those who learn
> may come to a full knowledge of your purposes
> revealed in your Son Jesus Christ;
> who is alive and reigns with you,
> in the unity of the Holy Spirit,
> one God, now and for ever.

READING   *Proverbs 8.22–31*

A reading from the Book of Proverbs.

> The LORD created me at the beginning of his work,
>   the first of his acts of long ago.
> Ages ago I was set up,
>   at the first, before the beginning of the earth.
> When there were no depths I was brought forth,
>   when there were no springs abounding with water.
> Before the mountains had been shaped,
>   before the hills, I was brought forth –
> when he had not yet made earth and fields,
>   or the world's first bits of soil.
> When he established the heavens, I was there,
>   when he drew a circle on the face of the deep,
> when he made firm the skies above,
>   when he established the fountains of the deep,
> when he assigned to the sea its limit,
>   so that the waters might not transgress his command,
> when he marked out the foundations of the earth,
>   then I was beside him, like a master worker;
> and I was daily his delight,
>   rejoicing before him always,
> rejoicing in his inhabited world
>   and delighting in the human race.

This is the word of the Lord.

EDUCATION

PSALM 111.1–2, 7–9a, 10

Teach us the way of your commandments.
All **Teach us the way of your commandments.**

I will give thanks to the Lord with my whole heart,
in the company of the faithful and in the congregation.
The works of the Lord are great,
sought out by all who delight in them.
All **Teach us the way of your commandments.**

The works of his hands are truth and justice;
all his commandments are sure.
They stand fast for ever and ever;
they are done in truth and equity.
All **Teach us the way of your commandments.**

He sent redemption to his people;
   he commanded his covenant for ever.
The fear of the Lord is the beginning of wisdom;
   a good understanding have those who live by it;
his praise endures for ever.
All **Teach us the way of your commandments.**

ACCLAMATION

Alleluia. **Alleluia.**
Speak, Lord, your servant is listening:
you have the words of eternal life.
Alleluia.

GOSPEL *John 7.14–18*

Hear the Gospel of our Lord Jesus Christ according to John.

> About the middle of the festival Jesus went up into the temple and began to teach. The Jews were astonished at it, saying, 'How does this man have such learning, when he has never been taught?' Then Jesus answered them, 'My teaching is not mine but his who sent me. Anyone who resolves to do the will of God will know whether the teaching is from God or whether I am speaking on my own. Those who speak on their own seek their own glory; but the one who seeks the glory of him who sent him is true, and there is nothing false in him.'

This is the Gospel of the Lord.

PRAYER OVER THE GIFTS

> Wise and gracious Father,
> open our hearts to delight in your wisdom,
> that through the bread and wine
>   we offer you in thanksgiving
> we may know Jesus Christ to be the Way,
>   the Truth and the Life,
> God, for ever and ever.

EDUCATION

PRAYER AFTER COMMUNION

>Father eternal,
>source of all wisdom and insight,
>may we who have been nourished
>   by these holy mysteries
>be schooled in the service of Christ,
>that conformed to his image
>our lives may tell of his truth and goodness,
>now and in all eternity.

23

The Medical Profession

Care for the sick is the responsibility of all Christians. In this votive we pray for all who have a particular vocation to minister to those who suffer in body, mind and spirit.

The liturgical colour is of the season.

COLLECT

> God of compassion,
> your anointed Son brought healing to those
>   in weakness and distress:
> strengthen by your life-giving Spirit
> all whom you call to serve in the medical profession,
> that by their ministries
> your people may be made whole
>   in body, mind and spirit;
> through Jesus Christ your Son our Lord,
> who is alive and reigns with you,
> in the unity of the Holy Spirit,
> one God, now and for ever.

THE MEDICAL PROFESSION

READING   *Ecclesiasticus 38.1–8*

A reading from the Book of Ecclesiasticus.

> Honour physicians for their services,
>   for the Lord created them;
> for their gift of healing comes from the Most High,
>   and they are rewarded by the king.
> The skill of physicians makes them distinguished,
>   and in the presence of the great they are admired.
> The Lord created medicines out of the earth,
>   and the sensible will not despise them.
> Was not water made sweet with a tree
>   in order that its power might be known?
> And he gave skill to human beings
>   that he might be glorified in his marvellous works.
> By them the physician heals and takes away pain;
>   the pharmacist makes a mixture from them.
> God's works will never be finished;
>   and from him health spreads over all the earth.

This is the word of the Lord.

AT ALL TIMES AND IN ALL PLACES

PSALM 36.5–10

    You, Lord, shall save both man and beast.
All **You, Lord, shall save both man and beast.**

    Your love, O Lord, reaches to the heavens
    and your faithfulness to the clouds.
    Your righteousness stands like the strong mountains,
       your justice like the great deep.
All **You, Lord, shall save both man and beast.**

    How precious is your loving mercy, O God!
    All mortal flesh shall take refuge
       under the shadow of your wings.
    They shall be satisfied with the abundance
       of your house;
    they shall drink from the river of your delights.
All **You, Lord, shall save both man and beast.**

    For with you is the well of life
    and in your light shall we see light.
    O continue your loving-kindness
       to those who know you
    and your righteousness to those who are true of heart.
All **You, Lord, shall save both man and beast.**

ACCLAMATION

> Alleluia. **Alleluia.**
> The Spirit of the Lord is upon me:
> because he has anointed me.
> **Alleluia.**

GOSPEL *Luke 4.16–21*

Hear the Gospel of our Lord Jesus Christ according to Luke.

> When Jesus came to Nazareth, where he had been brought up, he went to the synagogue on the sabbath day, as was his custom. He stood up to read, and the scroll of the prophet Isaiah was given to him. He unrolled the scroll and found the place where it was written:
> 'The Spirit of the Lord is upon me,
>   because he has anointed me
>   to bring good news to the poor.
> He has sent me to proclaim release to the captives
>   and recovery of sight to the blind,
>   to let the oppressed go free,
>   to proclaim the year of the Lord's favour.'
> And he rolled up the scroll, gave it back to the attendant, and sat down. The eyes of all in the synagogue were fixed on him. Then he began to say to them, 'Today this scripture has been fulfilled in your hearing.'

This is the Gospel of the Lord.

PRAYER OVER THE GIFTS

> Gracious Father,
> accept this offering which we place upon your altar:
> may it restore us to yourself
> and heal us by your Spirit;
> through Jesus Christ our Lord.

PRAYER AFTER COMMUNION

> Father eternal,
> may we who have known your healing love
> in broken bread and wine outpoured,
> strengthen those who suffer
>   with the hope of life made new
> in Jesus Christ our Lord.

PART THREE

Pastoral Ministry

24

Thanksgiving for Marriage

The Church believes that as a married couple 'grow together in love and trust, they shall be united with one another in heart, body and mind, as Christ is united with his bride, the Church'. In this celebration, the bride of Christ offers the Eucharist, the sacrament of Holy Communion, in thanksgiving for the gift of marriage, and in intercession for all married couples.

It may appropriately be used with couples shortly after their marriage (if the marriage itself was not celebrated within the context of the Eucharist), on anniversaries of marriage, and at other significant times.

In addition to the texts provided here, material from Common Worship: Times and Seasons, President's Edition for Holy Communion, *pp. 619–20, may be used.*

The liturgical colour is white.

COLLECT

> God our Father,
> we thank you for the gift of marriage,
> and those whom you have united within its bond.
> May their lives reveal your love for the world,
> that unity may overcome estrangement,
> forgiveness heal guilt,
> and joy overcome despair;
> through Jesus Christ your Son our Lord,
> who is alive and reigns with you,
> in the unity of the Holy Spirit,
> one God, now and for ever.

READING *1 John 4.7–12*

A reading from the First Letter of John.

> Beloved, let us love one another, because love is from God; everyone who loves is born of God and knows God. Whoever does not love does not know God, for God is love. God's love was revealed among us in this way: God sent his only Son into the world so that we might live through him. In this is love, not that we loved God but that he loved us and sent his Son to be the atoning sacrifice for our sins. Beloved, since God loved us so much, we also ought to love one another. No one has ever seen God; if we love one another, God lives in us, and his love is perfected in us.

This is the word of the Lord.

THANKSGIVING FOR MARRIAGE

PSALM 127

    Those who trust in the Lord shall not be put to shame.
All **Those who trust in the Lord shall not be put to shame.**

    Unless the Lord builds the house,
    those who build it labour in vain.
    Unless the Lord keeps the city,
    the guard keeps watch in vain.
All **Those who trust in the Lord shall not be put to shame.**

    It is in vain that you hasten to rise up early
    and go so late to rest, eating the bread of toil,
    for he gives his beloved sleep.
All **Those who trust in the Lord shall not be put to shame.**

    Like arrows in the hand of a warrior,
    so are the children of one's youth.
    Happy are those who have their quiver full of them:
    they shall not be put to shame
        when they dispute with their enemies in the gate.
All **Those who trust in the Lord shall not be put to shame.**

ACCLAMATION

    Alleluia. **Alleluia.**
    God is love, and those who live in love live in God:
    and God lives in them.
    Alleluia.

GOSPEL John 15.1, 4–6, 8

Hear the Gospel of our Lord Jesus Christ according to John.

> Jesus said to his disciples, 'I am the true vine, and my Father is the vine-grower. Abide in me as I abide in you. Just as the branch cannot bear fruit by itself unless it abides in the vine, neither can you unless you abide in me. I am the vine, you are the branches. Those who abide in me and I in them bear much fruit, because apart from me you can do nothing. If you abide in me, and my words abide in you, ask for whatever you wish, and it will be done for you. My Father is glorified by this, that you bear much fruit and become my disciples.'

This is the Gospel of the Lord.

PRAYER OVER THE GIFTS

> Gracious Father,
> as we offer the sacrifice of Jesus, the true vine,
> may those who have been joined together in marriage
> be renewed through his selfless love
> and abide in him for ever,
> to whom be ascribed all praise and glory,
> now and always.

PRAYER AFTER COMMUNION

> O God of love,
> you have nourished us with the gifts of redemption:
> may this foretaste of eternity
> increase our longing to feast at the
>   wedding banquet of heaven
> where with all the saints we will live for ever
>   to praise you;
> through Jesus Christ our Lord.

25

The Sick and Suffering

In this Eucharist we pray for the sick and all who suffer from any kind of need, that in Christ they may know healing, wholeness and peace.

In addition to the texts provided here, appropriate material from Common Worship: Times and Seasons, President's Edition for Holy Communion, *pp. 626–41, may also be used.*

The liturgical colour is of the season.

COLLECT

Loving God,
as a mother you are tender towards your children;
hear us as we pray for those who are sick and in need:
touch them with your renewing love
and uphold them by your Spirit,
that they may know healing in the wounds
   of Christ crucified,
who is alive and reigns with you,
in the unity of the Holy Spirit,
one God, now and for ever.

THE SICK AND SUFFERING

READING *Romans 8.18–23*

A reading from the Letter of Paul to the Romans.

> I consider that the sufferings of this present time are not worth comparing with the glory about to be revealed to us. For the creation waits with eager longing for the revealing of the children of God; for the creation was subjected to futility, not of its own will but by the will of the one who subjected it, in hope that the creation itself will be set free from its bondage to decay and will obtain the freedom of the glory of the children of God. We know that the whole creation has been groaning in labour pains until now; and not only the creation, but we ourselves, who have the first fruits of the Spirit, groan inwardly while we wait for adoption, the redemption of our bodies.

This is the word of the Lord.

PSALM 46.1–2, 4–5, 7a

> The Lord of hosts is with us.

All **The Lord of hosts is with us.**

> God is our refuge and strength,
> a very present help in trouble;
> Therefore we will not fear, though the earth be moved,
> and though the mountains tremble
>> in the heart of the sea.

All **The Lord of hosts is with us.**

There is a river whose streams make glad
   the city of God,
the holy place of the dwelling of the Most High.
God is in the midst of her;
   therefore shall she not be removed;
God shall help her at the break of day.

All **The Lord of hosts is with us.**

ACCLAMATION

Alleluia. **Alleluia.**
Come to me, all you that are weary
   and are carrying heavy burdens:
and I will give you rest.
Alleluia.

GOSPEL *Mark 6.54–end*

Hear the Gospel of our Lord Jesus Christ according to Mark.

When Jesus and his disciples got out of the boat, people at once recognized Jesus, and rushed about that whole region and began to bring the sick on mats to wherever they heard he was. And wherever he went, into villages or cities or farms, they laid the sick in the market-places, and begged him that they might touch even the fringe of his cloak; and all who touched it were healed.

This is the Gospel of the Lord.

PRAYER OVER THE GIFTS

> God of grace and goodness,
> accept all we offer you this day
> and through the bread and wine we bless and share,
> restore the sick to wholeness of life;
> through Jesus our Saviour and Lord.

PRAYER AFTER COMMUNION

> God of all compassion,
> by the dying and rising of your Christ
> you restore us to yourself
> and enfold us in your love.
> May we who have been refreshed
> with the bread of life and cup of salvation
> be renewed by your healing Spirit
> and be made ready for the coming of your kingdom;
> through Jesus Christ our Lord.

26

The Bereaved

St Ignatius of Antioch describes the Eucharist as the 'medicine of immortality'. In this votive we pray for the bereaved that hope in the resurrection of Christ may bring light out of darkness.

In addition to the texts provided here, appropriate material may also be used from Common Worship: Pastoral Services, *pp. 275–82;* Common Worship: Times and Seasons, President's Edition for Holy Communion, *pp. 621–5; and for the Commemoration of All Souls, from* Common Worship: Festivals, *pp. 188–93.*

The liturgical colour is of the season.

THE BEREAVED

COLLECT

Father in heaven,
sure refuge and strength in time of trouble,
hear the cry of those who mourn
 the loss of loved ones.
sustain them in their grief,
uphold them in despair,
and lighten their darkness with the hope of new life;
through Jesus Christ our risen Lord,
who is alive and reigns with you,
in the unity of the Holy Spirit,
one God, now and for ever.

READING 2 Samuel 18.24—19.4

A reading from the Second Book of Samuel.

David was sitting between the two gates. The sentinel went up to the roof of the gate by the wall, and when he looked up, he saw a man running alone. The sentinel shouted and told the king. The king said, 'If he is alone, there are tidings in his mouth.' He kept coming, and drew near. Then the sentinel saw another man running; and the sentinel called to the gatekeeper and said, 'See, another man running alone!' The king said, 'He also is bringing tidings.' The sentinel said, 'I think the running of the first one is like the running of Ahimaaz son of Zadok.' The king said, 'He is a good man, and comes with good tidings.'

Then Ahimaaz cried out to the king, 'All is well!' He prostrated himself before the king with his face to the ground, and said, 'Blessed be the LORD your God, who has delivered up the men who raised their hand against my lord the king.' The king said, 'Is it well with the young man Absalom?' Ahimaaz answered, 'When Joab sent your servant, I saw a great tumult, but I do not know what it was.' The king said, 'Turn aside, and stand here.' So he turned aside, and stood still.

Then the Cushite came; and the Cushite said, 'Good tidings for my lord the king! For the LORD has vindicated you this day, delivering you from the power of all who rose up against you.' The king said to the Cushite, 'Is it well with the young man Absalom?' The Cushite answered, 'May the enemies of my lord the king, and all who rise up to do you harm, be like that young man.'

The king was deeply moved, and went up to the chamber over the gate, and wept; and as he went, he said, 'O my son Absalom, my son, my son Absalom! Would that I had died instead of you, O Absalom, my son, my son!'

It was told Joab, 'The king is weeping and mourning for Absalom.' So the victory that day was turned into mourning for all the troops; for the troops heard that day, 'The king is grieving for his son.' The troops stole into the city that day as soldiers steal in who are ashamed when they flee in battle. The king covered his face, and the king cried with a loud voice, 'O my son Absalom, O Absalom, my son, my son!'

This is the word of the Lord.

THE BEREAVED

PSALM 23

    The Lord is my Shepherd, there is nothing I shall want.
All **The Lord is my Shepherd, there is nothing I shall want.**

    He makes me lie down in green pastures
    and leads me beside still waters.
    He shall refresh my soul
    and guide me in the paths of righteousness
        for his name's sake.
All **The Lord is my Shepherd, there is nothing I shall want.**

    Though I walk through the valley of the
        shadow of death,
        I will fear no evil;
    for you are with me;
        your rod and your staff, they comfort me.
    You spread a table before me
        in the presence of those who trouble me;
    you have anointed my head with oil
        and my cup shall be full.
All **The Lord is my Shepherd, there is nothing I shall want.**

    Surely goodness and loving mercy shall follow me
        all the days of my life,
    and I will dwell in the house of the Lord for ever.
All **The Lord is my Shepherd, there is nothing I shall want.**

ACCLAMATION

> Alleluia. **Alleluia.**
> Christ has been raised from the dead:
> the first fruits of those who have fallen asleep.
> **Alleluia.**

GOSPEL *John 14.1–6*

Hear the Gospel of our Lord Jesus Christ according to John.

> Jesus said to his disciples, 'Do not let your hearts be troubled. Believe in God, believe also in me. In my Father's house there are many dwelling-places. If it were not so, would I have told you that I go to prepare a place for you? And if I go and prepare a place for you, I will come again and will take you to myself, so that where I am, there you may be also. And you know the way to the place where I am going.' Thomas said to him, 'Lord, we do not know where you are going. How can we know the way?' Jesus said to him, 'I am the way, and the truth, and the life. No one comes to the Father except through me.'

This is the Gospel of the Lord.

PRAYER OVER THE GIFTS

> Accept, O gracious Father,
>   the gifts we offer on your altar:
> may the sacrifice of Christ
> which has removed the sting of death,
> bring hope to those who mourn
> and reveal to them the light of your presence;
> we ask this through Christ our Lord.

PRAYER AFTER COMMUNION

> Living Father,
> in this Eucharist you have nourished us with
>   the medicine of immortality
> and given us a foretaste of the heavenly banquet:
> as we believe in Christ's victory over death,
> so may we always rejoice in the
>   power of his resurrection,
> for he is our Lord and God, now and for ever.

27

The Homeless

In this Eucharist we pray for the homeless and dispossessed. As we recognize their need, the gospel challenges us to remember that whatever we do to the least of those who are members of Christ's family, we do to him.

The liturgical colour is of the season.

COLLECT

>Father eternal,
>whose infant Son was laid in a stable manger,
>strengthen and support those who are homeless;
>in the face of danger protect them from all harm,
>grant them security and shelter
>and give them hope in the knowledge that they are
>   your beloved children;
>through Jesus Christ our Redeemer and Lord,
>who is alive and reigns with you,
>in the unity of the Holy Spirit,
>one God, now and for ever.

THE HOMELESS

READING *Deuteronomy 15.7–11*

A reading from the Book of Deuteronomy.

> Moses said to all Israel: 'If there is among you anyone in need, a member of your community in any of your towns within the land that the LORD your God is giving you, do not be hard-hearted or tight-fisted towards your needy neighbour. You should rather open your hand, willingly lending enough to meet the need, whatever it may be. Be careful that you do not entertain a mean thought, thinking, "The seventh year, the year of remission, is near", and therefore view your needy neighbour with hostility and give nothing; your neighbour might cry to the LORD against you, and you would incur guilt. Give liberally and be ungrudging when you do so, for on this account the LORD your God will bless you in all your work and in all that you undertake. Since there will never cease to be some in need on the earth, I therefore command you, "Open your hand to the poor and needy neighbour in your land."'

This is the word of the Lord.

AT ALL TIMES AND IN ALL PLACES

PSALM 107.1–2, 4–7

Give thanks to the Lord for his goodness.
All **Give thanks to the Lord for his goodness.**

O give thanks to the Lord, for he is gracious,
for his steadfast love endures for ever.
Let the redeemed of the Lord say this,
those he redeemed from the hand of the enemy.
All **Give thanks to the Lord for his goodness.**

Some went astray in desert wastes
and found no path to a city to dwell in.
Hungry and thirsty,
their soul was fainting within them.
All **Give thanks to the Lord for his goodness.**

So they cried to the Lord in their trouble
and he delivered them from their distress.
He set their feet on the right way
till they came to a city to dwell in.
All **Give thanks to the Lord for his goodness.**

ACCLAMATION

Alleluia. **Alleluia.**
Just as you did it to one of the least of my
 brothers and sisters:
you did it to me.
Alleluia.

GOSPEL *Matthew 25.31–40*

Hear the Gospel of our Lord Jesus Christ according to Matthew.

> Jesus said to his disciples, 'When the Son of Man comes in his glory, and all the angels with him, then he will sit on the throne of his glory. All the nations will be gathered before him, and he will separate people one from another as a shepherd separates the sheep from the goats, and he will put the sheep at his right hand and the goats at the left. Then the king will say to those at his right hand, "Come, you that are blessed by my Father, inherit the kingdom prepared for you from the foundation of the world; for I was hungry and you gave me food, I was thirsty and you gave me something to drink, I was a stranger and you welcomed me, I was naked and you gave me clothing, I was sick and you took care of me, I was in prison and you visited me." Then the righteous will answer him, "Lord, when was it that we saw you hungry and gave you food, or thirsty and gave you something to drink? And when was it that we saw you a stranger and welcomed you, or naked and gave you clothing? And when was it that we saw you sick or in prison and visited you?" And the king will answer them, "Truly I tell you, just as you did it to one of the least of these who are members of my family, you did it to me."'

This is the Gospel of the Lord.

PRAYER OVER THE GIFTS

> Loving Father,
> in bread and wine we celebrate the presence
>   of your Son:
> help us to recognize the homeless as our
>   brothers and sisters
> and to serve Christ in them,
> who is our Lord and God, now and for ever.

PRAYER AFTER COMMUNION

> God our refuge,
> we thank you for feeding us at your table
> with gifts of grace and goodness:
> may we who are now sent out in your name
> stand alongside the homeless and dispossessed
> and enable them to find shelter
>   under the shadow of your wings;
> through Jesus Christ our Lord.

28

Victims of Natural Disaster

In this Eucharist we recognize that there are powerful forces within creation which bring devastation to the lives of many people. We pray for all victims of natural disaster, and those who seek to help and support them.

This votive is particularly appropriate in the days following a natural disaster, and in Christian Aid week.

The liturgical colour is of the season.

COLLECT

> God of mercy,
> when flood, storm and earthquake
>   scar the face of the earth,
> have compassion on all who suffer:
> calm their fears,
> heal their wounds,
> and be their eternal refuge;
> through Jesus Christ your Son our Lord,
> who is alive and reigns with you,
> in the unity of the Holy Spirit,
> one God, now and for ever.

READING   *Isaiah 54.9–10*

A reading from the prophecy of Isaiah.

> This is like the days of Noah to me:
>   Just as I swore that the waters of Noah
>   would never again go over the earth,
> so I have sworn that I will not be angry with you
>   and will not rebuke you.
> For the mountains may depart
>   and the hills be removed,
> but my steadfast love shall not depart from you,
>   and my covenant of peace shall not be removed,
>   says the Lord, who has compassion on you.

This is the word of the Lord.

PSALM   *121*

> Our help is in the name of the Lord.
All   **Our help is in the name of the Lord.**

> I lift up my eyes to the hills;
> from where is my help to come?
> My help comes from the Lord,
> the maker of heaven and earth.
All   **Our help is in the name of the Lord.**

VICTIMS OF NATURAL DISASTER

     He will not suffer your foot to stumble;
     he who watches over you will not sleep.
     Behold, he who keeps watch over Israel
     shall neither slumber nor sleep.
All   **Our help is in the name of the Lord.**

     The Lord himself watches over you;
     the Lord is your shade at your right hand,
     So that the sun shall not strike you by day,
     neither the moon by night.
All   **Our help is in the name of the Lord.**

     The Lord shall keep you from all evil;
     it is he who shall keep your soul.
     The Lord shall keep watch over your going out
        and your coming in,
     from this time forth for evermore.
All   **Our help is in the name of the Lord.**

ACCLAMATION

     Alleluia. **Alleluia.**
     Heaven and earth will pass away:
     but my words will not pass away.
     Alleluia.

GOSPEL   *Mark 13.1–8, 31*

Hear the Gospel of our Lord Jesus Christ according to Mark.

> As Jesus came out of the temple, one of his disciples said to him, 'Look, Teacher, what large stones and what large buildings!' Then Jesus asked him, 'Do you see these great buildings? Not one stone will be left here upon another; all will be thrown down.'
>
> When he was sitting on the Mount of Olives opposite the temple, Peter, James, John, and Andrew asked him privately, 'Tell us, when will this be, and what will be the sign that all these things are about to be accomplished?' Then Jesus began to say to them, 'Beware that no one leads you astray. Many will come in my name and say, "I am he!" and they will lead many astray. When you hear of wars and rumours of wars, do not be alarmed; this must take place, but the end is still to come. For nation will rise against nation, and kingdom against kingdom; there will be earthquakes in various places; there will be famines. This is but the beginning of the birth pangs.'
>
> 'Heaven and earth will pass away, but my words will not pass away.'

This is the Gospel of the Lord.

VICTIMS OF NATURAL DISASTER

PRAYER OVER THE GIFTS

Father all-powerful,
accept the bread and wine we offer on your altar.
When faith is shaken by disasters in this world,
assure us of your eternal presence
in Jesus Christ, our Saviour and Redeemer.

PRAYER AFTER COMMUNION

Tender God,
in this Eucharist you have brought us
   into communion
with those who suffer as a result of disaster:
uphold them in their hour of need,
strengthen those who toil to help them,
and give us all generous hearts to respond to the
   suffering of others.
This we ask through Christ our Lord.

29

Victims of War and Conflict

In this Eucharist we commend to God all victims of war, conflict and acts of terror, and commit ourselves to work to reveal God's reign of justice, mercy and peace.

This votive is particularly appropriate in the days before and after Remembrance Sunday, and during any conflict.

In addition to the texts provided here, appropriate material for Remembrance Sunday may be used from Common Worship: Times and Seasons, *pp. 573–85.*

The liturgical colour is of the season.

VICTIMS OF WAR AND CONFLICT

COLLECT

> God of love, whose compassion never fails;
> we bring before you
> the griefs and perils of peoples and nations;
> the necessities of the homeless;
> the helplessness of the aged and weak;
> the sighings of prisoners;
> the pains of the sick and injured;
> the sorrows of the bereaved.
> Comfort and relieve them, O merciful Father,
> according to their needs;
> for the sake of your Son, our Saviour Jesus Christ,
> who is alive and reigns with you,
> in the unity of the Holy Spirit,
> one God, now and for ever.

READING   *2 Samuel 1.17, 19–end*

A reading from the Second Book of Samuel.

> David intoned this lamentation over Saul and his son
>   Jonathan:
>   Your glory, O Israel, lies slain upon your high places!
>   How the mighty have fallen!
>   Tell it not in Gath,
>   proclaim it not in the streets of Ashkelon;
>   or the daughters of the Philistines will rejoice,
>   the daughters of the uncircumcised will exult.

AT ALL TIMES AND IN ALL PLACES

You mountains of Gilboa,
    let there be no dew or rain upon you,
    nor bounteous fields!
For there the shield of the mighty was defiled,
    the shield of Saul, anointed with oil no more.

From the blood of the slain,
    from the fat of the mighty,
the bow of Jonathan did not turn back,
    nor the sword of Saul return empty.

Saul and Jonathan, beloved and lovely!
    In life and in death they were not divided;
they were swifter than eagles,
    they were stronger than lions.

O daughters of Israel, weep over Saul,
    who clothed you with crimson, in luxury,
    who put ornaments of gold on your apparel.
How the mighty have fallen
    in the midst of the battle!

Jonathan lies slain upon your high places.
    I am distressed for you, my brother Jonathan;
greatly beloved were you to me;
    your love to me was wonderful,
    passing the love of women.

How the mighty have fallen,
    and the weapons of war perished!

This is the word of the Lord.

VICTIMS OF WAR AND CONFLICT

PSALM   20.1–2, 5, 7–8

>We will call on the name of the Lord.
>
>*All*   **We will call on the name of the Lord.**
>
>May the Lord hear you in the day of trouble,
>the name of the God of Jacob defend you;
>Send you help from his sanctuary
>and strengthen you out of Zion.
>
>*All*   **We will call on the name of the Lord.**
>
>May we rejoice in your salvation
>   and triumph in the name of our God;
>may the Lord perform all your petitions.
>
>*All*   **We will call on the name of the Lord.**
>
>Some put their trust in chariots and some in horses,
>but we will call only on the name of the Lord our God.
>They are brought down and fallen,
>but we are risen and stand upright.
>
>*All*   **We will call on the name of the Lord.**

ACCLAMATION

>Alleluia. **Alleluia.**
>Peace I leave with you:
>my peace I give to you.
>**Alleluia.**

GOSPEL *John 14.18–27*

Hear the Gospel of our Lord Jesus Christ according to John.

> Jesus said to his disciples, 'I will not leave you orphaned; I am coming to you. In a little while the world will no longer see me, but you will see me; because I live, you also will live. On that day you will know that I am in my Father, and you in me, and I in you. They who have my commandments and keep them are those who love me; and those who love me will be loved by my Father, and I will love them and reveal myself to them.' Judas (not Iscariot) said to him, 'Lord, how is it that you will reveal yourself to us, and not to the world?' Jesus answered him, 'Those who love me will keep my word, and my Father will love them, and we will come to them and make our home with them. Whoever does not love me does not keep my words; and the word that you hear is not mine, but is from the Father who sent me.
>
> 'I have said these things to you while I am still with you. But the Advocate, the Holy Spirit, whom the Father will send in my name, will teach you everything, and remind you of all that I have said to you. Peace I leave with you; my peace I give to you. I do not give to you as the world gives. Do not let your hearts be troubled, and do not let them be afraid.'

This is the Gospel of the Lord.

PRAYER OVER THE GIFTS

> Lord of heaven and earth,
> receive all that we offer you this day:
> may this Eucharist heal the scars of war
> and renew our hope in your promise of peace;
> through Jesus Christ our Lord.

PRAYER AFTER COMMUNION

> Father most merciful,
> you have fed us with the living bread
>   which brings life to the world:
> strengthened by your living presence,
> help us to overcome the powers of death and destruction
> and to bring in Christ's reign of justice and peace,
> who is our Lord and God, now and for ever.

30

The Departed

Every Eucharist brings us into communion with the whole Church, living and departed. In this votive we rejoice in the power of Christ's resurrection, and commend to God in prayer the souls of the departed. We pray that, at the last, we may come with them to feast at the banquet of heaven.

This votive may be used to commemorate one person, a group of people who have lost their lives, or the departed in general. It is appropriate in the days following a death, or on an anniversary.

In addition to the texts provided here, appropriate material may also be used from Common Worship: Pastoral Services, *pp. 275–82;* Common Worship: Times and Seasons, President's Edition for Holy Communion, *pp. 621–5; and for the Commemoration of All Souls, from* Common Worship: Festivals, *pp. 188–93.*

The liturgical colour is purple, black or white.

THE DEPARTED

COLLECT

Father of all,
we pray to you for [N and all] those we love,
   but see no longer.*
Grant them your peace,
let light perpetual shine upon them,
and in your loving wisdom and almighty power,
work in them the good purpose of your perfect will;
through Jesus Christ your Son our Lord,
who is alive and reigns with you,
in the unity of the Holy Spirit,
one God, now and for ever.

*This line may be adapted as appropriate.

READING   *Revelation 21.1–7*

A reading from the Revelation to John.

I, John, saw a new heaven and a new earth; for the first heaven and the first earth had passed away, and the sea was no more. And I saw the holy city, the new Jerusalem, coming down out of heaven from God, prepared as a bride adorned for her husband. And I heard a loud voice from the throne saying,
  'See, the home of God is among mortals.
  He will dwell with them;
  they will be his peoples,
  and God himself will be with them;
  he will wipe every tear from their eyes.
  Death will be no more;

mourning and crying and pain will be no more,
for the first things have passed away.'
And the one who was seated on the throne said, 'See, I am making all things new.' Also he said, 'Write this, for these words are trustworthy and true.' Then he said to me, 'It is done! I am the Alpha and the Omega, the beginning and the end. To the thirsty I will give water as a gift from the spring of the water of life. Those who conquer will inherit these things, and I will be their God and they will be my children.'

This is the word of the Lord.

PSALM 27.1, 4–6, 12, 17

Wait for the Lord;
be strong and he shall comfort your heart.
All **Wait for the Lord;
be strong and he shall comfort your heart.**

The Lord is my light and my salvation;
whom then shall I fear?
The Lord is the strength of my life;
of whom then shall I be afraid?
All **Wait for the Lord;
be strong and he shall comfort your heart.**

THE DEPARTED

One thing have I asked of the Lord
   and that alone I seek:
that I may dwell in the house of the Lord
   all the days of my life,
To behold the fair beauty of the Lord
and to seek his will in his temple.

All **Wait for the Lord;**
be strong and he shall comfort your heart.

For in the day of trouble
   he shall hide me in his shelter;
in the secret place of his dwelling shall he hide me
   and set me high upon a rock.

All **Wait for the Lord;**
be strong and he shall comfort your heart.

You have been my helper;
leave me not, neither forsake me,
   O God of my salvation.
I believe that I shall see the goodness of the Lord
in the land of the living.

All **Wait for the Lord;**
be strong and he shall comfort your heart.

ACCLAMATION

Alleluia. **Alleluia.**
This is the bread that came down from heaven:
the one who eats this bread will live for ever.
Alleluia.

GOSPEL *John 6.35–40*

Hear the Gospel of our Lord Jesus Christ according to John.

> Jesus said to the Jews, 'I am the bread of life. Whoever comes to me will never be hungry, and whoever believes in me will never be thirsty. But I said to you that you have seen me and yet do not believe. Everything that the Father gives me will come to me, and anyone who comes to me I will never drive away; for I have come down from heaven, not to do my own will, but the will of him who sent me. And this is the will of him who sent me, that I should lose nothing of all that he has given me, but raise it up on the last day. This is indeed the will of my Father, that all who see the Son and believe in him may have eternal life; and I will raise them up on the last day.'

This is the Gospel of the Lord.

PRAYER OVER THE GIFTS

> Gracious Father,
> eternal source of life and light:
> through the bread and wine we offer and receive,
> renew in us your promise
> to raise up those who have died,
> that they may hunger and thirst no more.
> This we ask through Christ our Lord.

PRAYER AFTER COMMUNION

God of love,
in this sacrament you have fed us with the bread of life:
welcome all who have been nourished at your
    table on earth
to the eternal banquet of heaven;
through Jesus Christ our Lord.

Resources

Extracts from the following source publications are listed in the Acknowledgements table on p. 173, alongside the numbered votives they appear in.

Official resources

Common Worship: Collects and Post Communions (CWCPC), Church House Publishing, 2004.

Common Worship: Festivals (CWF), Church House Publishing, 2008.

Common Worship: Pastoral Services (CWPS), Church House Publishing, 2005.

Common Worship: Services and Prayers for the Church of England (CWSP), Church House Publishing, 2000.

Common Worship: Times and Seasons (CWTS), Church House Publishing, 2006.

Common Worship: Times and Seasons, President's Edition for Holy Communion (CWTSPE), Church House Publishing, 2010.

New Patterns for Worship, Church House Publishing, 2008.

Supplementary resources

The Book of Common Prayer with the Additions and Deviations Proposed in 1928 (*BCP*), Oxford University Press, 1928.

The Book of Alternative Services of The Anglican Church of Canada (*BAS*), Anglican Book Centre, 1985.

Celebrating Common Prayer (*CCP*), Mowbray, 1992.

Colquhoun, F. (ed.), *Parish Prayers* (*PP*), Hodder & Stoughton, 1967.

Dix, G., *The Shape of the Liturgy*, Dacre Press, 1945; a new edition, with an introduction by Simon Jones, was published by Continuum in 2005.

Gordon-Taylor, B. and S. Jones, *Celebrating the Eucharist*, SPCK, 2005.

Hill, C. and E. Yarnold (eds), *Anglicans and Roman Catholics: The Search for Unity*, SPCK, 1994.

Jones, S., *The Sacramental Life: Gregory Dix and His Writings*, Canterbury Press, 2007.

Masses of the Holy House of Our Lady of Walsingham (*MOLW*), the Shrine at Walsingham.

The New English Hymnal (*NEH*), based on 273, William Bright, 'And now, O Father', Canterbury Press, 1986.

Opening Prayers: Collects in a Contemporary Language (*OP*) (International Commission on English in the Liturgy), Canterbury Press, 1999.

The Roman Missal (*RM*), Catholic Truth Society, 2010.

Temple, W., in Colquhoun, F. (ed.), *Parish Prayers*, Hodder & Stoughton, 1967.

Tristam SSF (ed.), *Exciting Holiness*, Canterbury Press, 2003.

Tristam SSF (ed.), *The Word of the Lord – Special Occasions*, Canterbury Press, 2001.

Acknowledgements

Votive	Collect	Acclamation	Prayer Over the Gifts	Prayer After Communion
1	OP (p. 52)*	Te Deum Laudamus	Jones from Te Deum	BAS (p. 347)*
2	CWSP (p. 420)	CWSP (p. 320)*	Jones	CWCPC (p. 165)
3	Jones	CWF (p. 103)	BAS (p. 423)*	CWF (p. 106)
4	BCP 1928 (p. 742)*	Philippians 2.10	Jones	Jones
5	CCP (p. 399)	Matthew 11.29 1 John 4.10 John 10.14	Jones	Jones
6	OP (p. 19)*	Luke 3.22	Jones based on NEH 273	Jones
7	OP (p. 54)*	John 6.48, 50, 58	RM (pp. 565 and 537)*	Jones from Aquinas
8	OP (p. 137)*	Luke 1.28, 42	Jones	Jones
9	MOLW*	Luke 1.38	Jones	CWSP (p. 379)
10	Jones	1 Peter 2.9	Jones	CWSP (p. 423)
11	CWF (p. 109)	Benedicite	RM (p. 675)*	CWF (p. 113)
12	Jones	John 17.21	Jones	CWTS (p. 145)
13	CWSP (p. 420)	Matthew 5.16	Jones	Jones

{ 173 }

14	Jones	John 15.16	Jones	*CWTS* (p. 641)
15	Jones	Psalm 85.12*	Jones	*CWCPC* (p. 168)
16	Jones	Matthew 5.9	Jones	*CWF* (p. 356)
17	William Temple (p. 275)*	Matthew 5.6	Jones	Jones
18	*RM* (p. 899)*	Matthew 20.28	Jones	Jones
19	William Temple (p. 277)*	Matthew 5.8	Jones	*CWF* (p. 365)
20	*CWSP* (p. 416)	Luke 15.24	Jones	Jones
21	*CWCPC* (p. 175)	Luke 22.25, 27	Jones	Jones
22	*CWCPC* (p. 163)*	1 Samuel 3.9; John 6.68 *CWSP* (p. 280)*	Jones	Jones
23	Jones	Luke 4.18a	Jones	Jones
24	*CWPS* (p. 157)*	1 John 4.16	Jones	Jones
25	Jones	Matthew 11.28	Jones	*CWPS* (p. 38)
26	Jones	1 Corinthians 15.20	Jones	Jones
27	Jones	Matthew 25.40	Jones	Jones
28	Jones	Mark 13.31	Jones	Jones
29	*PP* (p. 301)	John 14.27a	Jones	Jones
30	*BAS* (p. 429)	John 6.58	Jones	Jones

* = altered